Merry Christmas 1972

Mrs Dengler + Delores

AMAZING
BASEBALL
TEAMS

The stories of seven major league baseball teams, one selected from each decade of the Twentieth Century, and how they earned their distinction. Included are: the 1908 Chicago Cubs, the 1914 Boston Braves, the 1927 New York Yankees, the 1934 St. Louis Cardinals, the 1948 Cleveland Indians, the 1955 Brooklyn Dodgers, and the 1969 New York Mets.

AMAZING BASEBALL TEAMS

By DAVE WOLF

Illustrated with photographs

RANDOM HOUSE
NEW YORK

CONTENTS

INTRODUCTION

In the spring of 1962, before the New York Mets played their first game, Manager Casey Stengel bravely told a group of reporters, "Come on out to the Polo Grounds and watch my team. They're gonna be amazin'." Casey was right. The Mets were amazing—amazingly bad. The nickname stuck, however, and from then on people referred to them as the "Amazing Mets."

The Mets of 1969 were amazing, too. But, unlike their hilariously incompetent predecessors, they won the World Series.

The Mets are one of seven great teams, one from each decade of baseball's modern history, described in this book. Each ballclub was amazing in its own way. The 1908 Chicago Cubs, for instance, were part of a great dynasty which dominated the National League during the early years of the Twentieth Century. In 1908, they triumphed in the midst of bizzare circumstances, including baseball's most famous base-running blunder.

The 1914 Boston Braves, on the other hand, hardly possessed a victorious tradition. In fact, they were considered notorious losers, very much like the Mets. But in 1914 they overcame almost impossible odds to accomplish the sport's most remarkable comeback. The Braves were in last place on the Fourth of July, but they stormed back to win the pennant.

Many observers believe that the 1927 New York Yankees were the best team of all time. Led by Babe Ruth, they dominated the baseball world like no team, before or since.

The 1934 St. Louis Cardinals were amazing because of their style as well as their victories. The Cards were composed of uninhibited, rowdy players who specialized in tossing water bombs from windows and heckling their own manager.

The Cleveland Indians of 1948 were not a great team. They were a tribute to owner Bill Veeck, who built a losing team into a World Champion. At the same time, he proved himself to be baseball's most ingenious promoter as Cleveland set an all-time record for home attendance.

The 1955 Brooklyn Dodgers completely overwhelmed the rest of the National League and set many records on their way to the pennant. But the Dodgers had done that before. They were amazing in 1955 because they finally gave their loyal, zany, long-suffering fans a World Championship after years of frustrating Series defeats.

If there was a single common quality which marked all these teams, it was their intense determination to succeed. They were amazing for various reasons. But they were World Champions for one reason: the players on each team refused to accept anything less than victory.

AMAZING BASEBALL TEAMS

1908 Chicago Cubs

TINKER
TO EVERS
TO CHANCE

America was a bustling, growing nation in 1908. Although Oklahoma, Arizona, and New Mexico had not yet become states, America's center of population was shifting westward—transported by a vast railroad network and a new, inexpensive automobile called the "Model-T Ford."

The more the population moved west, the more Chicago became the center of the nation. Through the large, teeming city at the foot of Lake Michigan ran virtually all of the major East-West railroads and many of the North-South ones. The railroads brought cattle from the West, which in turn were slaughtered, packed and transported to the East and other points. Likewise, goods processed in the East passed through Chicago on the way west.

Chicago also had become the center of baseball, the young American game that had become the national pastime for millions of people. Chicago had been one of the earliest cities to sponsor a professional franchise. The city had entered a team in the National League when it was founded in 1876 and another in the American League upon its conception in 1901. From the 1880s on, Chicagoans were blessed with championship teams, whether the National League Cubs from the North Side of town, or the upstart American League White Sox from the South Side.

Baseball tightened its grip on Chicago, as well as the rest of the country, in 1903 when the rival American and National leagues entered into an agreement to hold a post-season championship—a World Series as it would be called. And for the decade that followed, no team dominated the game as consistently as the rough, rousing Cubs. From 1906 to 1911, the Cubs won four National League pennants, finished second twice, and won two World Series. By 1908 the Cubs were at the peak of their reign—and the entire baseball world was gunning for them.

No opponent, however, was more hostile in trying to upend the Cubs than the New York Giants. New York's manager, John J. McGraw, whose own team had won National League pennants in 1904 and 1905, frightened many clubs. He battled everyone from the league president down to the umpires. McGraw drove his players with such a ruthless, dictatorial fury that he became known as "Little Napoleon." He ordered his pitchers to brush back opposing batters with fastballs that grazed the hitters' heads. He instructed his players to slide into bases with spikes flying and to come up swinging at any opponent who dared to resist. The Giant players, fearing their "Little Napoleon" more than they feared the other teams, obliged.

But the Cubs were a fearless group in their own right. When the Giants used such tactics, the Cubs returned them—with something extra for good measure. Led by their great playing-manager, Frank Chance, the Chicago players were just as rough and rowdy as McGraw's New Yorkers.

In 1906, Chance's first full season as manager, the Cubs finished twenty games ahead of New York and actually walloped the Giants, 19-0, in one late-season game. That year they lost the World Series to their crosstown rivals, the White Sox. But the Cubs came back strong to win the 1907 pennant by seventeen games and take the World Series, too.

McGraw was almost hysterical with his desire for revenge. And in 1908 he came close to achieving it. But in one of the most exciting, vicious and bizarre pennant races of all time, McGraw met his match again.

The 1908 Cubs were truly a great team. First baseman Chance, second baseman Johnny Evers and shortstop Joe Tinker formed three-fourths of perhaps the most famous infield ever. All have since been elected to baseball's Hall of Fame in Cooperstown. In their own day, they were immortalized as Tinker-to-Evers-to-Chance, the greatest of double-play combinations. Actually the trio never set any records for double plays. The entire 1908 Chicago team, in fact, had only seventy-six, far short of the current major league record of 217. More significant, Tinker, Evers and Chance did not combine for a single double play during the two key games against the Giants, nor in any of the World Series games in 1908.

But, collectively, they did come up with some clutch double killings during the 1908 season and,

Shortstop Joe Tinker at bat.

Second baseman Johnny Evers.

First baseman Frank Chance.

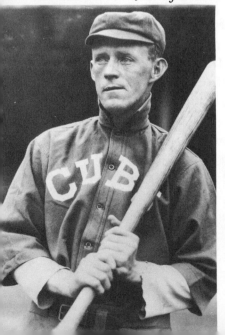

individually, they all justified their reputations as brilliant fielders. Undoubtedly, what immortalized them as a double-play combination were the words of a press-box poet named Franklin P. Adams. The New York sports columnist wrote:

These are the saddest of possible words,
  Tinker-to-Evers-to-Chance.
Trio of Bear Cubs fleeter than birds,
  Tinker-to-Evers-to-Chance.
Pricking our gonfalon bubble,
Making a Giant hit into a double,
Words that are weighty with nothing but trouble,
  Tinker-to-Evers-to-Chance.
                    —Baseball's Sad Lexicon.

Although Joe Tinker lacked ability with his bat, he made up for it with his glove. After joining the Cubs in 1902, he quickly established himself as one of the finest fielding shortstops in baseball. In 1908 he hit a fair .266. However, Joe did lead the Cubs in home runs. He had a grand total of seven! (The entire Chicago team combined for just twenty.)

Johnny Evers was a scrawny little fellow from Troy, New York. He had been working in a factory that made shirt collars at the turn of the century. When the plant went on strike, he begged for a try-out with the local minor league team. Most observers thought he was too small at just 135 pounds. But Evers got an opportunity and was so impressive that the major league Cubs bought his contract at the end of the season. He soon became the Cubs' spark plug. In fact, the hard-eyed, lantern-jawed Evers, who could do everything on a baseball field, earned the nickname "The Crab" from his teammates. In 1908, he led the Cubs in hitting with a .300 average and stole thirty-six bases.

Frank Chance was a brilliant leader of men. The Cubs called him "Husk," because of his strong, 200-pound build. Sportswriters often referred to him as "The Peerless Leader." A former catcher, the thirty-year-old Chance was an excellent fielder at first base. He had a lifetime batting average of .296, though his 1908 mark was somewhat lower at .272. Obviously he led by example. But Chance also led with his quick mind and powerful personality. He had to. The Cubs were a wild, undisciplined bunch. They were always fighting their opponents—and often they were fighting among themselves. Tinker and Evers stopped talking to each other in 1908. "Every time something went wrong on the field," Evers admitted later, "we would be at each other and there would be a fight in the clubhouse. He'd rush at me and get me by the throat and I'd punch him in the belly and try to cut him with my spikes." One player even tried to maim Tinker with a pair of first-aid scissors during a locker-room argument.

But Chance somehow kept the men under control. He had a temper of his own and the Cubs knew about it. Once after a thirteen-game winning streak came to an end, Chance threw a bat through a piano and tossed every table in sight out of the clubhouse. The Cubs also learned that Chance had at one time been a top amateur boxer in California. His code was simple: "You do things my way or meet me after the game."

But Chance could be a sensitive man, too. After

Powerful Frank Chance led by example—on and off the field.

fining one player $2,500 during the course of the season for various violations, Chance turned the money over to the player's wife. "It was the only way the poor girl would ever get anything," he said.

The players also respected Chance's judgment on the field. It was he who devised the play to break up the sacrifice bunt with men on first and second. Shortstop Tinker would hold the runner at second close to the base by threatening a pickoff play. When the bunt came, the pitcher would cover the third base line. Chance would come in from first and cover his side of the field. Meanwhile, the third baseman would stay close enough to the base to take the throw from either Chance or the pitcher. And since the runner at second had been kept near the base before the pitch, the Cubs were often able to make the force play at third. Big leaguers still use this strategy.

The pipe-smoking son of a bank president, Chance owned a percentage of the Cubs. He bought into the franchise in 1906 when they set a record for victories—116—that still stands. Toward the end of the season, owner Charles Taft was very impressed by a single play in which Chance, using heads-up base running, scored from second on a bunt. He called Chance into his office. "Any manager with the brains to do what you did," said Taft, "deserves more than a salary. How would you like to buy ten per cent of the Cubs?"

Chance wrote a check for $10,000. Seven years later he sold his investment for $140,000. Certainly the broad-shouldered Chance was responsible for a large part of the Cubs' increase in value. But so were Tinker and Evers and the other key members of this marvelous club—Mordecai "Three Finger" Brown, Orval Overall, Ed Reulbach, Harry Steinfeldt, and Johnny Kling.

Brown, Overall, and Reulbach combined with a fourth starting pitcher, Jack Pfeister, to win eighty of the ninety-nine Cub victories in 1908. Brown was the ace of the staff. A tall, handsome man, he had acquired his nickname from a childhood accident in which half of the index finger on his pitching hand was destroyed. This forced him to throw with just three fingers. But three were apparently enough. From 1906 to 1911, Brown averaged more than twenty victories a year. In 1908, he posted a 27-9 record.

Steinfeldt was the forgotten member of the great infield. But the hard-nosed third baseman was very much a star in his own right. After spending much of the 1890s touring Texas with a minstrel show, he joined the Cincinnati Reds. But when he and the Reds had a salary disagreement, Steinfeldt stubbornly sat out part of two seasons. The Reds were happy to trade him after the 1905 season—and the Cubs were equally happy to get him. Steinfeldt led the Cubs with a .327 average in 1906. He hit only .241 in 1908, but he regularly knocked in runs in the clutch and tightened the infield with his powerful throwing arm.

Catcher Johnny Kling was one of the best of his era. Fast enough to steal sixteen bases, Kling hit a solid .276 in 1908 and handled the pitching staff with authority.

With Chance, the "Peerless Leader," guiding the team, it became a Series winner in 1907. And with Chance again driving the team relentlessly in 1908, the players had no opportunity to become complacent. One letup and the 1908 Cubs might have fallen out of the pennant race.

The race was a three-way battle almost from the season's start in April. In the early stages, the Cubs led. But, as the days of summer grew hotter, so did the competition. The Pittsburgh Pirates, led by shortstop Honus Wagner, and the Giants, led by pitcher Christy Mathewson, nipped at Chicago's heels. The Pirates took the lead in July. By August, the Giants were in first place. No team could gain a commanding margin.

The heated pennant race built up attendance

throughout the National League. Even the American League fans seemed to show more interest in the three-way National League struggle than they did in their own teams. On August 24 the crowd watching an American League game in New York demanded that the umpires delay the contest while time was taken to properly cheer the National League Giants, whose victory had just been posted on the scoreboard.

In late August, Chicago swept a three-game series from New York, but the Giants refused to fold. They quickly regained the lead. Then on September 4, the Cubs lost a game to the Pirates. Strangely enough Chicago's defeat that day may ultimately have saved the pennant for the Cubs.

The score was 0-0 in the last of the ninth when Pittsburgh got runners on first and third. The next Pirate batter singled to drive in the winning run. But the runner on first, as was the custom with all players at that time, didn't bother with the formality of touching second base. As soon as his teammate touched home, he stopped running the bases and headed for the dugout. Noticing what the base runner had done, Evers signaled to outfielder Solly Hofman to throw him the ball. Evers took the throw, tagged second, and claimed that the runner on first had been forced out, thus nullifying the winning run. The umpire, Hank O'Day, told Evers he was crazy.

But Evers informed Chance of the incident. The manager quietly protested the game to Harry Pulliam, president of the National League. Pulliam refused to wipe out the Pirates' victory. But he con-

Rivals McGraw, left, and Evers have a friendly meeting before a game. Few of their games were friendly, though.

ceded that the Cubs' protest had merit. At the same time, O'Day had been having second thoughts on the play. The rule—"No run can score when the final out of an inning is a force play"—had always been on the books. It simply had never been enforced. O'Day decided to call it the next time the play occurred.

All this was temporarily forgotten in the excitement of an eleven-game Giant winning streak. Then on September 18, New York swept a doubleheader and the Cubs, despite excellent pitching by Overall, lost to Philadelphia. The Giants appeared to be pulling away. In the gloomy Chicago clubhouse, Tinker approached Chance. "Well, Skipper, I guess that does it," Tinker said sadly. "Why don't we make a night of it?"

Chance's eyes flashed. "No," he snapped. "We

were good winners last year and the year before. Let's show them we can be good losers and play the string out. We might win it yet."

The next day Three-Finger Brown overpowered the Phillies, 4-2, while Pittsburgh broke the Giants' winning streak. When the Pirates beat New York again and Chicago won a doubleheader the following afternoon, the complexion of the race suddenly began to change.

The Cubs moved into the Polo Grounds, New York's home field, for the most important series of the season. They had to keep winning—and they did. Brown saved the opener of a doubleheader in relief. Then, in the clubhouse between games, Chance handed Brown a new ball. "Go out and warm up," he said. "You're starting the second one." Brown went all the way to win, 3-1.

This set the stage the next day for one of the memorable events in baseball history. McGraw, angry that his lead was slipping away, started the Giants' ace winner, Mathewson. Chance countered with Jack "The Giant Killer" Pfiester, a pitcher without an awesome win-loss record but a man who had particularly good success against the New Yorkers.

The game was scoreless until the fifth inning when Tinker, who for some unknown reason always hit well against Mathewson, slashed a sinking line drive to right field. "Turkey Mike" Donlin tried to make a diving shoe-string catch. But he missed. As 25,000 rabid Giants fans—a huge crowd in 1908— moaned, the ball rolled past the sprawling Donlin.

Tinker circled the bases for an inside-the-park home run.

Donlin redeemed himself in the next inning, however, when he singled in a run to tie the score. From then on, both Mathewson and Pfiester were almost flawless. The Giants could hardly hit a ball out of the infield. Tinker handled fourteen chances and Evers eleven. But the Cubs could do no better against the Giants' great right-hander. When New York came up in the last of the ninth, the score was still 1-1.

Art Devlin singled for the Giants with one out, but Moose McCormick forced him at second for out number two. Pfiester appeared safe. The next batter was nineteen-year-old rookie Fred Merkle, playing his first full major league game at first base. Merkle surprised everyone by slapping a single that sent McCormick to third. When Al Bridwell followed with a line drive hit to center, the Giants appeared to have won the crucial game.

As McCormick trotted across the plate, the fans raced onto the field to mob Bridwell and the Giants But Johnny Evers had noticed something: In the confusion, Merkle hadn't bothered to touch second base. New York's first-base coach had run onto the field and thrown his arms around the rookie first baseman as soon as Bridwell singled. Then, to avoid the fans, they had raced together toward the clubhouse in deep center field.

Solly Hofman had fielded Bridwell's hit in right center. Seeing Evers perched on second, where he was screaming for the ball, Hofman threw hurriedly toward the infield. But his throw was wild. It skipped past Tinker and Evers and rolled behind third base. Joe McGinnity, the Giants' veteran pitcher, was coaching third. (Players often served as coaches, too, in baseball's less formal years.) Realizing that something was wrong, McGinnity ran for the ball. Just as he pounced on it, Tinker and Evers grabbed him. They wrestled for the ball, but the powerful McGinnity broke free and threw the ball into the crowd.

A whirlpool of confusion followed. There are several versions of what happened next. The Giants claimed the ball disappeared into the crowd. The Cubs, they said, then took a ball from the ballbag on their bench, and threw it to Evers. Johnny always denied the charge.

"I can still see the fellow who caught McGinnity's throw," Evers said, years later. "A tall, stringy middle-aged gent with a brown bowler hat on. Steinfeldt and Floyd Kroh, a young pitcher of ours, raced after him. . . . The guy wouldn't let go of the ball. But suddenly Kroh solved the problem. He hit the customer right on top of that stiff hat and drove it down over his eyes. As the gent folded up, the ball fell free and Kroh got it. I was yelling and waving my hands by second base and Tinker relayed it over to me and I stepped on the bag and made sure the umpire saw me."

The umpire was Hank O'Day. He had not forgotten his blunder in Pittsburgh nineteen days earlier. "He's out," O'Day shouted above the noise of the crowd. "The run does not count."

Bedlam broke loose all over the field. O'Day, realizing that it would be impossible to clear the field of angry fans, declared the game a 1-1 tie. McGraw fumed. He kept hollering that the Giants had won. The fans, who thought the Cubs were trying to pull some trick, gave the Cubs a good going over.

The controversy lasted for days. McGraw howled that it was unfair to suddenly enforce the rule and demanded that New York be awarded the victory. He also, rightfully, defended Merkle. The first baseman went on to have a fine career, but he never did live down the memory of his "bonehead play." Actually he was a victim of circumstance, for he had only done what all the other players usually did.

McGraw took his protest to the league presi-

One "bonehead" play spoiled Fred Merkle's career.

dent, Pulliam. But Chance also lodged a protest. He argued that when O'Day called Merkle out, the game was still in progress. Since it was impossible to clear the field and since the home team—New York, in this case—was responsible for keeping order, Chance argued further that the Cubs should be declared winners by legal forfeit. The baseball hierarchy rejected both protests and supported O'Day. The game would be replayed the day after the season ended, if necessary.

As it turned out, the replay was necessary. The race remained so tight that a single defeat often dropped a team from first to third. The Cubs traveled to Brooklyn after the protested game and won, 5-1. The next day they moved into first place as pitcher Ed Reulbach staged a truly astonishing performance. At the time, it wasn't unusual for a pitcher to start both games of a doubleheader. And indeed the strong-armed Reulbach, who was on his way to a 24-7 record and 298 innings pitched for the season, could handle the chore. But Reulbach not only won both games, he pitched two shutouts. The feat has never been matched—before or since. In eighteen innings, Reulbach gave up just eight hits.

Nevertheless, the Cubs could not stay ahead. When they took the field against the Pirates on October 4 for their final regular-season game, the pennant was hanging in the balance. Chicago trailed Pittsburgh by a half game. If the Cubs lost, they were finished. If they won, they would eliminate Pittsburgh but would still have to contend with

New York. The Giants had three games left on their schedule.

Mordecai Brown, who had started or relieved in eleven of the Cubs' previous fourteen games, carried the team once more. Chicago won, 5-2. The Cubs' last scheduled game had been played. Now they had to wait to see what would happen to the Giants.

New York won all three of its remaining games, giving the Cubs and Giants identical 98-55 records. Thus the two teams found themselves replaying the disputed game in New York in order to settle the pennant fight.

If the blood had seemed bitter between the Cubs and Giants in the past, it was boiling over now. Both McGraw and his Giants, as well as their fans, believed Evers had "stolen" the pennant. In the hotel on the day of the big game, Johnny's telephone rang constantly. "They [the Giant fans] said that if I played, they would kill me," he revealed. "They said they'd cut my ears off and send them to my mother."

Mordecai Brown was also threatened. He arrived at the park with a half-dozen poison-pen letters in his pocket. The message was always the same: "We'll kill you if you pitch and beat the Giants."

Few games have ever attracted as much interest. The press box at the Polo Grounds was so crowded that writers were almost sitting on each other's laps. Throughout the country, fans crowded around telegraph offices, waiting for scores. The largest crowd ever to see a baseball game up to that time—more

Pitcher Mordecai Brown proved that he was a lot tougher than the men who made threats against him.

than 35,000—arrived early. The Polo Grounds stopped selling tickets hours before the game, but thousands who had tickets couldn't force their way through the mobs that clogged the streets outside. Even the Cubs, who arrived in horse-drawn carriages, had a rough time getting into the park. The umpires arrived an hour late.

The bluffs overlooking the Polo Grounds were packed with people. The elevated train could not run because fans were sitting on the tracks, from which they could see the park. Fights broke out in the stands as ticket holders arrived to find their seats occupied. The left-field fence was set ablaze and thousands charged through. In frustration, the fire department turned its hoses on the rowdy fans.

The Cubs came out for batting practice amidst a shower of bottles, cushions, garbage and verbal abuse from the stands. "I never heard any set of men called as many foul names as the Giant fans called us," said the usually hard-bitten Brown.

Ten minutes before the game, as the teams exchanged heated insults, Mathewson made his majestic entrance. Wearing a long white linen "duster"— like those used by auto drivers in those days—he left the clubhouse and walked very slowly toward the mound. With every step he took, the cheering grew louder. Matty had already won thirty-five games that season. The fans were pleading for just one more.

Meanwhile, there was trouble under the stands. Dr. William Creamer, the Giants' unofficial team physician, was trying to bribe Umpire Bill Klem The previous evening, Creamer had attempted to thrust a fistful of bills into Klem's hand while the umpire was walking down a dark street. Now, as Creamer approached Klem again, the umpire slammed him to the ground. Creamer had no bet on the game; he was just an overzealous fan. (Although he claimed he was innocent, Dr. Creamer was later barred from baseball for life.)

When the game finally began, the Giants seemed ready to break it open in the first inning. After Mathewson had easily retired the Cubs, Pfiester—

the Chicago starter—hit the first batter and walked the next. Then the Cubs got a break. Pfiester struck out Roger Bresnahan. When Cub catcher Johnny Kling dropped the third strike, Buck Herzog, the Giant runner on first, foolishly broke for second— and was thrown out. Even that couldn't save Pfiester. "Turkey Mike" Donlin hit a double, driving in a run and sending the stands into an uproar. A fireman watching the game from a telephone pole behind the fence became so excited he fell off and was hospitalized.

Pfiester walked the next batter and was taken out. Brown, who had been warming up in the bullpen, was called upon to replace Pfiester. Brown grimly fired a final warm-up pitch, whirled and began to push his way through the hostile crowd that covered the grass in deep right.

"Get out of my way," he roared. "Here's where you 'poison pen' guys get your chance. If I'm going to get killed I sure know that I'll die before a capacity crowd."

Brown struck out the next batter to retire the side and end the Giant threat. The Cubs rallied in the third. Tinker lined a triple over the center fielder's head. Kling singled to tie the score. After two outs, Cub outfielder Frank Schulte doubled to send Chicago ahead, 2-1.

After another Cub reached base, Manager Chance was in a position to widen the lead. Ignoring the loud and bitter boos, he slashed a double to right, driving in two more vital runs. The Cubs had a 4-1 lead.

In the seventh inning, the Giants made a desperate bid to score. They got two singles and a walk from Brown. The bases were loaded with none out. McGraw sent in tough Larry Doyle to hit for Mathewson. Brown worked carefully. Doyle popped a high foul near the stands. As Kling moved under it, the exasperated fans threw hats, bottles and papers into the air to distract him. But he made the catch —one out.

After a sacrifice fly had scored a second run for New York, Herzog hit a sizzling ground ball up the middle. It appeared to be a sure single. But Tinker darted over, knocked the ball down and threw out Herzog. The side was retired, the threat was over, and Chicago still had the lead, 4-2.

As Chicago took its two-run lead into the last of the ninth and the Giants' hopes waned, the mood of the fans became increasingly hostile. But Brown refused to let up. He had allowed just one run since the first inning. With two out he forced Devlin to hit a grounder to shortstop. Tinker scooped it up and threw to Chance for the final out. The Cubs had won their third straight pennant.

The bitter Giant fans charged onto the field, intent on taking out their frustrations on the Cub players. The Chicagoans began sprinting for the far-off clubhouse. Some were caught and beaten by the mob. Pfiester was slashed with a knife. Chance was hit in the throat and remained hoarse until halfway through the World Series. The police had to draw their guns to keep the fans from breaking down the Cubs' clubhouse door.

After the Cubs' ordeal in New York, the Detroit Tigers—even with tough, mean Ty Cobb leading them—could hardly be expected to intimidate the Chicago veterans in the World Series. They didn't.

Chance hit .421 and stole five bases against the Tigers. Brown and Overall each won two games. The Cubs won the Series easily, four games to one. They were champions of the world. And they had earned their victory the hard way.

1914 Boston Braves

THE MIRACLE BRAVES

One morning in May, 1914, veteran pitcher Hub Perdue looked at the National League's standings and shook his head. "It's hard to figure how there could be a ballclub rottener than some of the ones we've played against," he said with a laugh. "But one club is rottener—and we're it!"

Hub Perdue's club was the Boston Braves. At the time he made his comment, their record was four wins–eighteen losses, and they were in last place. Most people, including Perdue, felt certain the Braves would remain at the bottom for the rest of the season.

But 1914 was a year of startling developments. In Detroit, automobile manufacturer Henry Ford agreed to double his workers' pay from $2.50 to $5 a day. In Latin America, the first ship sailed through the Panama Canal—an inland waterway which engineers had said could never be built. In Europe, where peace had reigned for over forty years, an archduke was assassinated and World War I began. It was only appropriate that something amazing should happen on the baseball field, too.

The site of this incredible miracle was Boston. There the Braves—a ragtag collection not unlike the original New York Mets—rose from last place in mid-July to win the pennant in early October. It was, up to that time, the most remarkable comeback in major league baseball.

The Braves were unlikely champions. They had only three good pitchers. Their hitting was so weak that just one Brave batted over .300. Most of the players had come to Boston after having been discarded by other teams. But somehow these greatest of all underdogs kept outhustling, outfighting and outsmarting every opponent in the league. By the end of the season they had accomplished the impossible and earned the title, "The Miracle Braves."

The story of the "Miracle Braves" began on a cold, gray September day at New York's Polo Grounds in 1912. The Braves were completing their season some fifty-two games behind their host, the league-leading New York Giants. In the stands sat James Gaffney, the Braves' owner. He was tired of watching his team lose. Four years in a row, they had come in last.

Sitting with Gaffney was George Stallings, the man who had already been signed as Boston's manager for 1913. Stallings watched in utter disbelief while the Giants humiliated the Braves. The Boston players, he thought to himself, were lazy, incapable and careless.

Finally Gaffney turned to Stallings. "Well, what do you think?" he asked.

Stallings looked his new boss in the eye. "I've been stuck with some terrible teams in my day," he answered, "but this one beats them all."

Manager George Stallings, right, of the Braves had to face Giant Manager McGraw, left, with an inferior team.

"I know it," replied Gaffney. "But that's why we hired you. You are the absolute boss. I want you to run the club as if it were your own. I want a winning team."

Stallings' task appeared hopeless. The Braves were known everywhere as the worst team in the major leagues. But Stallings had actually gone after the job. Although he owned a large plantation in Georgia and was well off financially, he wanted more than anything to prove himself as a big league manager. A minor league catcher during his playing days, Stallings had managed in the majors for five years. He was widely respected as a man who could improve weak clubs. But none of his teams had ever won a pennant.

Off the field, Stallings was a fashionably dressed gentleman. At the ballpark his character changed. Few managers were as fiery or hot-tempered. Stallings argued endlessly with umpires. And his booming voice heaped scorn and sarcasm upon any player who made a careless error.

Though the 46-year-old Stallings was a brilliant strategist, he is best remembered as a handler of men. Nothing, he felt, was more important than the morale of his players. His motto was simple: "You *can* win. You *must* win. You *will* win!"

"Give me a ballclub of only mediocre ability and, if I can get the players in the right frame of mind, they'll beat the world champions," he often said. "But they've got to believe they can do it."

When Stallings took over the Braves in 1913, he began trading players as though they were bubble-gum cards. He didn't want pompous stars. Stallings looked for men who could be taught the value of intelligent, hustling play. By the end of his first season, the results were obvious. Boston had climbed to fifth place. When the 1914 campaign opened, Stallings felt that his team had a good chance to finish in the first division.

Then, to his dismay, the Braves fell apart. The Brooklyn Superbas battered them, 8-2, on opening day. From then until June 25, when the Boston team escaped from the cellar for a mere twenty-four hours, the Braves were entrenched in last place. Stallings' pitchers couldn't get the ball over the plate. When they did, opponents belted it out of the park. His hitters had even worse problems. Once again the Braves were the laughing stock of the National League.

"This bunch of mine is the worst-looking club I've ever seen," Stallings said in May. "They can't do anything right. But I've never seen such lousy luck as we've been having. It'll take a month to get us back in shape, but then we're going to be hard to beat."

The month passed and Boston was still losing, but at least the Braves began to look better. Many of their defeats were the result of bad luck, not bad play, and many of their losses were by just one run. Two of their best players, shortstop Walter "Rabbit" Maranville and second baseman Johnny Evers, had come back in the lineup after early-season illnesses.

The 22-year-old Maranville was a happy-go-lucky little fellow. Just five feet, five inches tall, with a weight of 140 pounds, he looked more like a jockey than a professional ballplayer. But he was a

"Rabbit" Maranville hopped all over the infield to get ground balls. He hit surprisingly well, too, for his size.

brilliant fielder and a favorite of the fans. Baseball gloves of his day were scarcely more than small, floppy pieces of leather. They lacked both the deep pocket and wide webbing of those worn by today's fielders. Yet Maranville would range far and wide to stab grounders or bound into short left field to grab pop-ups with an exciting "basket" catch, much like the one used later by Willie Mays.

The Rabbit would do anything for a laugh. One day, after umpire Bill Finneran called a strike against him, Maranville took a pair of glasses from his pocket, polished them and handed them to the infuriated umpire. Another time, in Philadelphia, some of the Braves were playing cards in their hotel room. Suddenly one of the men cried out as he looked up at the window. The others turned in astonishment to see the Rabbit making faces at them through the glass. He was kneeling on a narrow ledge that ran around the hotel—twelve floors above the street!

The other Boston star, Johnny Evers, had come to the Braves from Chicago. The star second baseman on the Cubs' 1908 pennant winner, Evers had been named Chicago's playing-manager in 1913. Although the Cubs finished third, owner Charles Murphy foolishly took away the managerial part of Evers' job when the Cubs lost a post-season exhibition series to the Chicago White Sox. Evers was furious. He wanted to leave Chicago.

Stallings saw his chance. He traded his second baseman, Bill Sweeney, and a considerable amount of money for "The Crab." Then he gave Evers a $25,000 bonus. The money was well spent. Evers was Stallings' kind of ballplayer. A smart, rugged opportunist, he hated defeat as much as his manager did. Stallings appointed the thirty-one-year-old Evers as his captain on the field. Between these two perfectionists no Brave escaped criticism for long. "He'd make you want to punch him in the nose," Maranville said of Evers. "But you knew Johnny was thinking only of the team."

Aside from Evers and Maranville, Stallings' roster was filled with journeymen ballplayers and untried youngsters. His catcher, big Hank Gowdy, had flopped with the Giants, who were convinced

Gowdy was lazy and uncoordinated. At first base was rookie Butch Schmidt, a huge man who never hit with power. The third baseman was Charlie Deal, a slick fielder who couldn't hit hard enough to break a window. Deal had already been dropped by the Tigers.

The outfield was a dumping ground for failures from other teams. Stallings was so desperate he used eleven outfielders in 1914. Youthful Leslie Mann couldn't hit a curve ball. Swift Josh Devore, who had been discarded by the Giants and Philadelphia Phillies, couldn't hit left-handed pitching. Ted Cather and George "Possom" Whitted were St. Louis Cardinal rejects. Herb Moran had failed with three other teams. Even Joe Connolly, a fine hitter who started most of the games in left field, had a problem. He was such a bad defensive player that he had once been knocked out by a line drive.

By July, Stallings was using only three starting pitchers—Bill James, George Tyler and Dick Rudolph. James had great potential. He weighed 200 pounds and could throw as hard as anyone in the league. But every pitch was an adventure. No one—including James—seemed to know where the ball was going. When the season opened, James was still learning to control his spitball. The pitch was legal in those days, but James couldn't get it over the plate. Tyler was another hard thrower, but the left-hander couldn't control his pitches. He had lost forty-nine games during the previous three seasons. Rudolph had come from the Giants. John McGraw, the tough New York manager, had made up his mind that Rudolph, who stood five feet, eight

Stallings relied upon a three-man pitching staff when the pennant race heated up. With him, from the left, is the trio of Dick Rudolph, George Tyler, and Bill James.

inches tall and weighed 160 pounds, was too small for the big leagues.

With this motley crew, the Braves fell fifteen games behind the league-leading Giants after celebrating the Fourth of July by losing a doubleheader to Brooklyn. To make matters worse, the last-place Braves then went off to Buffalo, where they somehow lost an exhibition game to a soap company team.

Stallings suffered through each defeat, sliding nervously up and down the bench so many times he wore holes through five pair of pants. But he never gave up on his players. Instead he drove the team furiously, forcing his men to play heads-up ball and drilling them in the fundamentals of the game. Each morning, while other clubs slept in their hotels, Stallings held "skull session" meetings. There he went over every detail of the previous game, lashing the Braves for mental errors and explaining proper techniques and strategy. The manager also ordered lengthy pre-game workouts, during which he constantly reminded his players of the proper cutoff positions for throws from the outfield and the exact spot to place a bunt.

During games Stallings bellowed angry criticisms. The poor Braves became so accustomed to his bitter cracks that once when Stallings shouted, "Bonehead, get up there and see if you can hit the ball," seven players stepped to the bat rack. Each man thought the Boston manager was talking to *him*.

Stallings demanded complete dedication. Pitcher Hub Perdue learned this lesson the hard way. Perdue was pitching badly in 1914. But his hitting was even worse. "You've got to change your batting style," Stallings told him. "But you're so awful I don't know where to start. It's up to you."

The next day Perdue decided to play a joke on his manager. He batted right-handed his first time up and struck out. The next time he struck out batting left-handed. He then struck out right-handed again and completed his performance by taking the first strike from the right side of the plate, the second from the left, and the third from the right. "What in the name of heaven are you doing?" Stallings screamed.

"I just followed orders," Perdue said with a grin.

"You told me to change my batting style and I did!" Stallings didn't think it was very funny. Perdue was traded to the St. Louis Cardinals that night.

Slowly the downtrodden Braves absorbed Stallings' spirit. They began to play smart, aggressive baseball. When someone committed an error and Stallings shouted "Bonehead," the players on the bench started shouting right along with their manager. By the second week in July, Maranville and Evers were healthy and hitting well. Gowdy was throwing out base runners and handling the pitchers skillfully. Schmidt wasn't hitting homers, but his base hits had begun driving in runs. Stallings had also acquired slugging third baseman "Red" Smith from Brooklyn. Smith and Connolly gave the Braves a pair of solid power hitters.

But Boston's greatest asset was its three-man pitching staff. No manager had ever before been successful using just three starting pitchers for an extended period. Nevertheless, Stallings tried it. Tyler, James and Rudolph rotated, pitching every third game, often with only two days' rest. It was a gamble. But the gamble paid off. Tyler and James were finally getting the ball over the plate. James had mastered a fast spitball which few batters could touch. He was also acquiring control. "I learned my great lesson early," he said. "A pitcher can't get very far on speed alone."

Rudolph had no speed at all. But, during his short stay with the Giants, he had studied the way the great Christy Mathewson threw a curve ball. Now, after years of work, Rudolph could throw it almost as well. He combined the curve with perfect control

The Braves' best hurler, Dick Rudolph, had little speed on his pitches but his curve hooked around opposing batters.

to make himself the best pitcher on Stallings' staff.

Until the first week in July, the National League race had appeared dull. The Giants seemed headed toward their fourth straight pennant. Fans were losing interest. Attendance throughout the league was low. Most people preferred to spend the warm summer days riding in open-air trolley cars or just sitting close to their new electric fans.

Then suddenly the Braves began to win. On July 19 they swept a doubleheader in Cincinnati and va-

cated the cellar. "Now we'll catch New York," Stallings roared in the noisy locker room. "We're playing
thirty-three per cent better ball than any other team
in the league. They won't be able to stop us."

Boston, however, was still in seventh place.
Only Stallings' players took him seriously.

From Cincinnati, the Braves traveled to Pittsburgh, where their three-man pitching staff kept the
winning momentum alive. The hitters went into a
slump, but Tyler, James and Rudolph combined for
four shutouts in five games. In one contest the score
was 0-0 in the ninth. Then Maranville proved to
Stallings that he could be brave as well as funny.
With the bases loaded and two out, he leaned over,
allowing a fastball to strike him in the forehead. It
was a crazy play—but it worked. Umpire Charlie
Moran stared incredulously at the Rabbit as he
lay on the ground. "If you can walk to first, I'll let
you get away with it," he said at last. Dizzily,
Maranville staggered to first, where he was replaced by a pinch runner. The runner on third was
forced across the plate and Boston won, 1-0.

The Giants were still far ahead in the league, but
the rest of the seven teams were closely bunched.
Three days after leaving last place, the Braves
vaulted to fourth. Gaffney, the owner, was so delighted that he immediately signed each player to a
1915 contract.

The Braves continued to win. On August 6 in Bos-
ton, Maranville belted a rare home run. (The
Braves hit only thirty-five all season long.) The
Rabbit's blast carried Boston to a 5-4 victory over
Pittsburgh. The Braves had crept to within six and a

half games of New York. The unpredictable Braves were capturing the hearts of people all over the nation. Their game results were sharing front-page headlines, providing a little relief from the disturbing news of America's increasing involvement in the European war.

Although no one really thought that Stallings' team could win the pennant, many baseball fans were tired of brash John McGraw and his haughty Giants. They had their fingers crossed for the Braves. After a while the support for the Bostonians began to tell on the Giants. "We got discouraged," recalled New York catcher "Chief" Meyers in later years. "Everybody in the country seemed to be pulling for the Braves and against McGraw."

As the race grew more frantic, Stallings—who would dash across a street filled with traffic rather than walk under a ladder—became increasingly superstitious. He believed that trash left on the field would bring misfortune. So his players spent hours policing the grounds, and opponents delighted in watching him churn as they intentionally dropped little pieces of paper in front of Boston's dugout.

Stallings had another strange superstition. No matter what the position of his body when the Braves began a rally, he would not move a muscle until the inning was over. One day Boston went on a hitting spree just as the manager was bending over to tie his shoe laces. The rally lasted thirty-three minutes. When Stallings finally straightened up, he was so stiff he had to be helped to the locker room.

Victory followed victory. Each day another Brave player came through in the clutch. Luck was with the Boston team, too. Somehow their opponents were forever making costly errors, or the Braves' pop flys managed to drop in for hits.

In mid-August Boston roared into the Polo Grounds and won three straight from New York. By August 23, the Braves had caught up with the Giants. The two teams were tied for first place. Boston had wiped out a fifteen-game lead in only five weeks.

"Just look at that gang of misfits," moaned McGraw. "Isn't it the dumbest looking ballclub you ever saw? But they're winning the pennant."

For two weeks the Braves bounced in and out of first place. On Labor Day, when the Giants came into Boston to begin a three-game series, the teams were tied. McGraw was sure the moment had arrived for his team to knock Stallings' upstarts out of the race.

Single morning and afternoon games had been scheduled for Labor Day. Gaffney, the Braves' owner, shifted the contests from Boston's tiny, outdated South End Grounds to Fenway Park, home of the American League Boston Red Sox. Still there were not enough seats, and thousands stood on the fringes of the outfield. The combined two-game attendance was 74,163.

The Braves entered the ninth inning of the morning game trailing, 4-3. With Mathewson pitching for the Giants, many fans thought they were about to see Stallings' "Miracle" come to an end. But the Braves came charging back—just as they had done for the past two months. Devore beat out an infield roller and Moran slashed a double into the overflow crowd in right. Now it was up to Evers. He blooped a double to left, sending both runners across the plate. The happy crowd blanketed the field.

But Boston had not yet beaten the Giants. The New Yorkers rebounded in the afternoon to crush the Braves, 10-1. It was a wild game. In the midst of a four-run sixth inning, New York's centerfielder Fred Snodgrass became involved in a huge rhubarb. After Boston's Tyler almost hit him with a fast ball, Snodgrass reached first by intentionally allowing a pitch to graze his arm. The fans, already disappointed by the Giants' lopsided victory, were furious. Their anger multiplied when Snodgrass stood on first and thumbed his nose at Tyler.

When Snodgrass went to center field after the inning, the fans began to bombard him with pop bottles. Then Boston's mayor, James Curley, the Braves' loudest rooter, climbed from his box seat and strode onto the field. Waving his arms and shouting at the top of his lungs, His Honor tried to persuade the umpire, and then a police lieutenant, to throw Snodgrass out of the game for inciting a riot. The umpire and policeman refused. But McGraw—fearful that the fans might lynch Snodgrass on the spot—removed him from the game.

That afternoon was the last the Giants saw of first place. The next day Boston began its last furious drive to the pennant. James fired his spitball past the helpless New Yorkers, and the Braves wrapped up the game with four runs in the fourth inning. The Giants appeared shaken and demoralized. McGraw didn't even take his familiar place in the third-base coaching box. Now even he seemed to sense the impending "Miracle." James pitched a three-hitter as Boston won, 8-3. They were in first place to stay.

Relaxed and confident, the Braves roared down the home stretch and broke the race wide open in mid-September by winning ten games in a row. They clinched the pennant on August 29—exactly two years from the day Gaffney and Stallings had sat watching the Giants slaughter the Braves at the Polo Grounds.

Boston finished ten and a half games ahead of second-place New York. After losing forty of their first sixty-six, the Braves won fifty-two of their last sixty-six. Tyler, Rudolph and James pitched eighteen shutouts in the second half of the season. Rudolph, the man McGraw had called "too little," led the league in victories with twenty-seven. At one point he won twelve games in a row. Tyler finished with sixteen wins. James's record was 26-7; he won nineteen of his last twenty decisions.

Although he hit just .279, the scrappy Evers was voted the Most Valuable Player in the league and received a Chalmers automobile. Connolly led the team in hitting with a .306 average. Schmidt hit .285 and knocked in seventy-one runs. Red Smith, who batted .314 during his half-season with Boston, had eighty runs batted in. Cather hit .287.

But the "Miracle" was not yet complete. In the World Series, the Braves confronted the world champion Philadelphia Athletics, the great power of the American League. Managed by the famed Connie Mack, and boasting what was known as "The $100,000 Infield," they had just won their fourth pennant in five years. Their pitching staff included two future Hall of Fame members, "Chief" Bender and Eddie Plank, plus a youthful fast-baller, "Bullet" Joe Bush. Most of the experts still believed Stallings' club had been lucky to win the pennant, and they were convinced the Braves had only a slim chance in the Series. To make things worse, Red Smith was out of the Series with a broken ankle. Even Stallings was worried. But he kept his doubts to himself.

Groping for every psychological advantage he could, Stallings tried to unsettle the proud Athletics by predicting Boston would win in four games. Then he announced that Philadelphia was so weak he hadn't even bothered to have them scouted. Actually his scouts had been watching the Athletics for weeks. At secret meetings the Braves were told about more than the playing weaknesses of their opponents. Stallings was preparing for a war of nerves against the A's, and he made sure his men knew all the Philadelphians' personal problems and foibles. This, he felt, would make them better bench jockeys.

The Braves played best when they were angry. So Stallings continued to build up a feud with the A's. Two days before the opening game, he told Boston reporter Walter Hapgood, "I want to get their goats. I'm going to call all the writers to my room for a press conference. After a few minutes I want you to ask me when the Braves will practice tomorrow."

When the reporters assembled and Hapgood asked the question on cue, Stallings casually replied, "At two o'clock."

"But the Athletics practice at two," said a startled Philadelphia writer. Stallings quickly picked up the telephone and called Mack.

"Connie," he said in a friendly tone, "I was wondering about practice tomorrow. I figure on taking my boys on the field about two o'clock."

On the other end of the line, the gentlemanly Mack was trying to explain what Stallings already knew: that the A's were scheduled to practice at two and that Boston could have the field at any other time. Finally Stallings shouted, "But I don't want the field at noon or at four. I want it at two. Out of common decency to a visitor, I'd have changed things to suit you. . . . Well, you can have the field at two, and at noon, and at four too. We'll beat you four straight." With that he hung up on the bewildered Mack.

The next morning, just as Stallings had planned, newspapers in Boston and Philadelphia carried huge, front page headlines: BRAVES FIND SHIBE PARK CLOSED TO THEM FOR PRACTICE. MACK TURNS DOWN BRAVES.

As he had done throughout the season, Stallings fired up his team while they waited to go out for the Series opener.

"Hank Gowdy," he snapped. "The Giants didn't want you. Do you remember that?"

"Dick Rudolph. Everyone said you're too small. What are you going to do about it?"

"The A's are a *wonder team*," Stallings added sarcastically. "They're too good to beat, we're told. Well, I've said we'll win in four straight. Now make me right!"

The Braves were confident and snarling. When Maranville's friend, Athletic outfielder Eddie Murphy, trotted over to say hello before the game, the Rabbit turned his back sharply and walked away. The Braves even refused to dress at Shibe Park, home of the A's. Instead they used the Phillies' locker room at Baker Field several blocks away. Stallings added to the feud by chasing the public-address announcer out of the dugout when the poor fellow came in search of the starting lineup.

Mack tried to make Stallings believe he was going to start left-handed Eddie Plank when he really intended to use right-handed Chief Bender. Plank took batting practice. But Stallings was not fooled. Leaving nothing to chance, he had both a lefty and a righty pitch to his starters in batting practice. Thus the Braves were warmed up for either type of pitching.

Stallings' pre-Series tactics worked. Boston ripped the favored A's to shreds in the first game. They pounded Bender with a barrage of hits. Gowdy, who had batted only .243 during the regular season, had a single, double and triple. Rudolph pitched a five-hitter and the Braves won, 7-1.

The Athletics were, nevertheless, a great team. To beat them, the scrambling Braves needed the same kind of luck they had had during their run to the pennant. The second game was tied, 0-0, in the ninth when weak-hitting Chuck Deal, playing third in place of Smith, hit a fly to right. Amos Strunk misjudged the ball and Deal was on second with a double. As James fanned for the second out, the A's catcher fired a pick-off throw to second. Deal was trapped off the base. But instead of trying to dive back, he startled the A's by breaking for third and sliding in ahead of the throw. A bad play was converted into a stolen base. When Mann singled, Boston led, 1-0.

In the last of the ninth James, although pitching a two-hitter, began to weaken. With one out, the Braves' pitcher walked two men in a row. At the plate stood Eddie Murphy, who was so fast he had not grounded into a double play all year. "Get closer to the bag," Evers snapped at shortstop Maranville.

"I'm almost standing on it," protested the Rabbit.

"Well," growled Evers, "then get right on it!"

Murphy lined the next pitch between James's legs. It seemed a sure hit. But there was Maranville straddling the bag. The ball hopped into his glove. The startled Rabbit stepped on second and threw to first for a double play, ending the game.

To show his men how much confidence he had in them, Stallings ordered that all the Braves' equipment and road uniforms be taken home from Philadelphia. "We won't be coming back," he cried. "It'll all be over after two games in Boston."

With 35,000 hysterical fans packed into Fenway Park in Boston, the Braves won the third game, 5-4, in twelve innings. Gowdy belted two doubles and a home run. Stallings knew, however, that the Athletics still had the strength to bounce back. But he wanted his players to think otherwise. He canceled the Braves' train reservations to Philadelphia for the fifth game.

Fortunately, he never had to regret it. In the fourth game, Rudolph scattered seven hits. Evers broke a 1-1 deadlock in the fifth inning with a two-run single and the unbelievable Boston Braves won, 3-1. It was the first four-game sweep in World Series history.

The "Miracle" was complete. Through hustle, stubborn determination and great desire—plus an ample measure of luck—George Stallings and his horde of castoffs were champions of the baseball world.

Three seasons later, Schmidt, Connolly, Devore, Cather and James had all disappeared from the majors. Evers was a substitute, Rudolph had posted his last winning record and Stallings was again managing a second-division team. It would take thirty-four years for the Braves to win another pennant. But no one could ever take away their "Miracle."

1927 New York Yankees

MURDERERS' ROW

In 1927 the United States was a prosperous country. Her citizens earned good incomes. Many of them invested confidently in the stock market. Along with money for the usual necessities, they still had a good deal left to spend on fun and entertainment. Thus it was a frolicking, boisterous era—the peak of a decade called The Roaring Twenties.

Sports also flourished in the 1920s. The decade is still referred to as America's Golden Age of Sports. Anyone seeking heroes who personified success had dozens to choose from in the sports world, including "Red" Grange, Knute Rockne, Bill Tilden, Jack Dempsey and Bobby Jones. In baseball there were Babe Ruth and Lou Gehrig and, for that matter, the whole 1927 New York Yankee team. To this day, most baseball experts acknowledge the '27 Yankees as the greatest team ever assembled.

New York clinched the pennant earlier than any other team on record. The Yankees won 110 games and lost just forty-four. Finishing nineteen games ahead of the second-place Philadelphia Athletics, they swept the World Series in four straight games.

Either man by man, or as a whole, the 1927 Yan-

Manager Miller Huggins, center, may have put together the greatest team ever in 1927. Among his stars, from left to right, were Waite Hoyt, Babe Ruth, Bob Meusel, and Bob Shawkey.

kees possessed the finest talent in baseball. Four pitchers won eighteen games or more. Five men batted over .300. The Yanks recorded a .307 team average, one of the few teams ever to bat over .300. Four Yankees knocked in 100 or more runs. The team total of 158 home runs was nearly *three times better* than any other single club in the American League.

The Yankees' regular lineup was so devastating that it became known as "Murderers' Row." The name was more than a catchy phrase for sportswriters and fans to use. It was a reality for hapless opponents, who knew that every man in the

With the Boston Red Sox, Babe Ruth was a pitcher.

Yankee batting order was a threat to pound a pitcher off the mound.

The greatest of the Yankee sluggers, of course, was Ruth. Big George Herman "Babe" Ruth set records that still stand—most prominent is his 714 lifetime home run record.

Babe actually came into the American League as a pitcher for the Boston Red Sox in 1914. From 1914 until 1919, he was one of the best hurlers in the game. The boyish-faced left-hander won eighty-nine games and lost only forty-six. In one World Series he pitched twenty-nine consecutive scoreless innings, setting a record that lasted for forty-three years. But Babe was such a powerful hitter that his team couldn't afford to keep him out of the lineup every day. So he was shifted to the outfield, virtually full time, in 1919.

The following season, the Red Sox sold Babe to the Yankees for the unheard-of price of $125,000.

But Ruth proved to be worth ten times that much to the Yankees. His booming bat helped transform the New York team from a chronic loser into the most powerful team in the majors. More important, Ruth revolutionized baseball. Until Babe emerged, few players hit home runs. No manager counted on the long ball as part of his offense. The kind of ball being used was still "dead" (it didn't travel very far when it was hit).

However, Ruth was so powerful he knocked the so-called dead ball over fences for home runs. In 1918, even though he was still primarily a pitcher, he tied for the league lead with eleven home runs. The next year he spent most of his time in the outfield and hit twenty-nine home runs. Team owners and league officials quickly recognized that the home run added new excitement to the game and attracted more fans. They decided to get rid of the dead ball by replacing it with a livelier ball. The yarn was bound more tightly so that the new ball had more bounce when it was hit. Ruth responded to the change by smashing out fifty-four home runs in 1920. The following season he smacked fifty-nine.

Although Ruth was establishing himself as a living legend, he was not merely a slugger. He was a fine all-around hitter and fielder. In fact, his lifetime batting average—.342—was, and still is, the envy of the best of singles hitters. He could bunt or slap a hit into the opposite field. A graceful outfielder, despite his pudgy build, he possessed an excellent throwing arm.

Ruth was undoubtedly the country's most popular athlete. He was also baseball's highest paid player.

Ruth became a national celebrity. Here, he visits the White House, where he was the guest of the President.

His annual salary totaled more than $80,000. But the Babe was also a high-living fellow who kept the fans laughing with his off-field antics. Once a policeman stopped Ruth when Babe's car was barreling down a one-way street in the wrong direction.

"This is a one-way street," admonished the policeman.

"But officer," Ruth explained, "I was only going one way!"

Another time, when President Calvin Coolidge came out to the ball park in Washington, the Yanks lined up for formal introductions to the President. As Mr. Coolidge walked down the row, each Yankee said respectfully, "How do you do, Mr. President."

When Mr. Coolidge approached Babe, however, he simply stuck out his hand and said, "Mr. Ruth."

Babe took off his cap, wiped his forehead and said most informally, "Hot as hell, ain't it, Prez?"

But on the field, Ruth usually stuck to business. In 1927 he had his greatest year. He set baseball's most famous record by belting sixty home runs in a 154-game season. He also had a batting average of .356 and knocked in 164 runs.

Ruth, however, was only a part of the wondrous 1927 Yankee team. At first base was Lou Gehrig, in his third season as a starter but already regarded as baseball's second leading slugger. Lou had been discovered at Columbia University. He was a quiet, intelligent man who had practiced long, painful hours to overcome his weaknesses as a fielder. Seemingly immune to injury, Gehrig set a record by playing in 2,130 consecutive games. His lifetime batting average was .340. In 1927 Gehrig combined with the more flamboyant Ruth in baseball's most feared slugging tandem. Lou hit forty-seven home runs, batted .373 and set a league record with 175 runs batted in. Lou's performance was so impressive

Lou Gehrig boomed his hits almost as far as Ruth's.

that in 1927 he was voted the Most Valuable Player in the league, despite the Babe's sixty home runs.

Tony Lazzeri, the second baseman, was a tall, fiery youngster who in one season had hit sixty home runs in the minor leagues. Grim and silent, he always seemed ready to explode. "Interviewing that guy," said one reporter, "is like trying to mine coal with a nail file." But Lazzeri was poised and consistent on the field. His flawless fielding and his hitting would have made him the top threat on almost any team except the mighty Yankees. Tony hit .309 and slammed eighteen home runs in 1927.

Lazzeri's doubleplay partner was shortstop Mark Koenig. Mark was a slick fielder who played with a scrappy, aggressive style. Sometimes he was inconsistent and temperamental. But the cool, grim Lazzeri was always there to calm Koenig down. Although the Yankees considered Koenig one of the weakest links in their batting order, he hit a solid .285 in 1927.

Third baseman "Jumping Joe" Dugan rounded out the Yanks' excellent defensive infield. He had been a big league star for ten years, and was still a solid fielder in 1927. Although he never had a high batting average, he was a smart, experienced hitter in the clutch. Joe got his nickname while playing with the Philadelphia Athletics. He had a way of jumping very high to spear line drives. He also frequently "jumped" the ballclub. Joe considered Philadelphia a pretty dull town and he was forever taking off for a few days' vacation in the middle of the season. But Dugan liked life in New York. After joining the

Yankees in 1922, he confined his jumping to the playing field.

The Yankee outfield was one of the finest ever assembled. Each man was a superb fielder. Next to Ruth, who played right field, was swift center fielder Earle Combs. The lanky Combs was an ideal leadoff man because he got on base so often. He could spray the ball to all fields and he usually totaled at least 200 hits a season. Combs didn't hit with power, but he was an excellent bunter and base runner. Combs joined the Yankees in 1924 with the reputation of being a great base stealer in the minor leagues. But Miller Huggins, the Yanks' tough little manager, quickly let him know that power, not speed, was New York's primary weapon.

"I hear you are pretty fast," Huggins said to Combs upon meeting him.

"I don't know about that," the rookie answered with a confident grin, "but down in Louisville they called me the 'Mail Carrier.' "

"That's good," snapped Huggins, "because up here, Combs, we'll call you the 'Waiter.' We've got guys like Babe Ruth who can hit the ball a long, long way. You just get on base and *wait* for them to knock you in."

Combs took Huggins at his word. He didn't try to steal many bases, but he was constantly on base—ready and waiting for the Yankee sluggers to drive him across the plate. He had his finest season in 1927 when he batted a resounding .356 and made one sensational catch after another in center field.

Left fielder Bob Meusel hit .337 and batted in

103 runs in 1927. He was one of the best clutch hitters on the club and his throwing arm was regarded
as the finest in baseball. Bob was a reserved individual who wasn't especially friendly with the other
players. But despite this his teammates were happy
to have him on their side.

The Yankees' catching situation was never stable.
Johnny Grabowski, Benny Bengough and Pat Collins alternated at the position. None of them was an
especially good hitter, but Huggins shuttled them
in and out of the lineup in order to get the best performance out of each man. At the end of the season,
the combined batting average of the three catchers
was a respectable .275.

Pitchers who wore the Yankee uniform appre-
ciated what it meant to play for a team that had
Ruth, Gehrig and Meusel in the lineup. "The secret
of success as a pitcher," said Waite Hoyt, New
York's top hurler, "lies in getting a job with the Yankees. No pitcher with the Yankees should ever hold
out. If he did, he might get traded and then he
would have to pitch against them."

For all its modesty, however, the Yankee pitching
staff was the best in the league. Hoyt, who later
became a popular broadcaster for the Cincinnati
Reds, developed a sore arm early in the 1927 season,
but he finished the season with a 22-7 record. Urban
Shocker, a 37-year-old veteran, was one of the last
legal spitball pitchers. The spitball had been out-
lawed in 1920, but any pitchers using the pitch at
the time were allowed to continue throwing it until
they retired. Shocker, who had been a consistent
winner for more than a decade, had another fine

season in 1927. He used his wisdom and cunning to compile an 18-7 record. Herb Pennock, who had suffered from a lack of control early in his career, was the toughest left-handed pitcher in the league. Though 34 years old in 1927, he pitched with the enthusiasm of a teenager. His record was 19-7.

The Yankees' second-line pitching was also impressive. For instance, young George Pipgras, who was called up from the minors at the start of the season, was used in carefully chosen spots by Huggins and had a 10-3 record. "Dutch" Ruether, a crafty left-hander whom the Dodgers had given up on three years before, made a comeback with the Yankees. In 1927, his last good year, Ruether had a 13-6 record.

Whenever the starting pitchers faltered, Huggins simply turned to the bullpen and called on Wilcy Moore, an aging rookie who had never dreamed he would be pitching in the major leagues. Moore had labored in the minor leagues for six seasons without attracting the attention of any big league teams. Pitching for Greenville in the lowly South Atlantic League in 1926, Moore had won thirty games and lost only four. But when the season was over he decided that he was wasting his time as a minor league pitcher. He told his teammates that he was going home to his farm in Arkansas. He was finished with baseball.

But suddenly Wilcy Moore's life changed. The Yankees bought his contract, and Moore was invited to spring training. There he surprised everyone by not only making the team, but becoming the Yanks' best relief pitcher.

"I didn't know that anybody from the Yankees had looked at me in Greenville," he said later. "I didn't know they'd ever heard of me. Maybe it just happened—or maybe they were keeping it as a surprise for me. Anyway, I thought I'd come up and see what it was like in them ol' major leagues."

No one was certain about Moore's true age. But everyone agreed that he was older than the twenty-eight years he claimed to be. His age, however, was unimportant. It was his sinker ball that counted. The batters just couldn't hit this pitch—which was fortunate for Moore since it was his only effective one. Wilcy used to beg Manager Huggins to let him throw curve balls. Huggins would always reply with a laugh: "Your curve ball wouldn't go around a button on my vest." In other words, Wilcy's curve ball didn't curve—which made it a very easy pitch to hit.

Moore was a great relief pitcher in 1927. His record was 19-7 and his earned run average of 2.28 was the best in the league. Wilcy never seemed to be affected by pressure. But he was a terrible hitter. Although his swing was just fine, he always swung the bat in the same spot—no matter where the ball was pitched. Ruth often teased Moore about his lack of batting skill. Finally Babe bet Wilcy $300 to $100 that Moore wouldn't get five hits all season. With that Wilcy got lucky. Five times the opposing pitcher happened to throw the ball in the only spot where Moore could possibly have hit it. As a result, Wilcy got his five hits. Babe paid off the bet, and Wilcy used the $300 to buy two mules for his farm. Appropriately, he named them Babe and Ruth.

Miller Huggins got very little credit for the success of the Yankees. Some people felt that a five-year-old boy could have managed such a great team and still have won the pennant. At the time Huggins took over the Yankees in 1918, however, they had never won a pennant. Along with General Manager Ed Barrow, Huggins reshaped the club. Then the fiery leader and shrewd strategist piloted the Yankees to the pennant in 1922 and a pennant and World Series victory in 1923.

But the team slipped to second in 1924 and down to seventh in 1925. Many players, especially Babe Ruth, seemed to be working harder at night-time partying than they were at day-time ball-playing. Ruth's home-run production went down; his weight skyrocketed up. Finally Huggins really cracked down on his carefree stars. He levied heavy fines on many players. In late August of 1925, he had his confrontation with Ruth.

The Babe had arrived at the clubhouse thirty minutes late. Huggins was waiting for him.

"Where have you been?" snapped the manager.

"Oh," said Ruth casually, "I had some personal business to attend to."

"It seems," said Huggins, "that you've had a lot of personal business to attend to lately."

The Babe just shrugged his shoulders, gave a hearty yawn and continued pulling on his uniform. "Don't bother to put on that uniform," Huggins said coldly. Ruth looked up in surprise. "That's right," Huggins said again. "Don't bother to put on that uniform."

Ruth still didn't take his tiny manager seriously.

"Don't try to make a mug out of me, Hug," he laughed. "If you weren't such a little squirt, I'd smack you."

Suddenly Huggins took a deep breath, rose up to his full five-feet three-inches, and shouted, "No, I couldn't make a mug out of you if I tried. God did that a long time ago. I'm not afraid of you either. If I weighed forty pounds more I'd tan your hide. But for now, you are finished. You're suspended."

"You must be crazy," Ruth yelled.

Huggins ignored him. "And moreover, I'm fining you $5,000."

This was the largest fine in baseball up to that time. It was more than many players earned in a year. But Huggins made the fine stick and Barrow backed him up. Finally Ruth and his carousing teammates got the message. Though Babe didn't act like a saint thereafter, he did stay in good condition. And he apologized to Huggins. From this incident there grew a great bond of mutual respect and affection between Ruth and his manager.

During 1926, Huggins shook up the club by trading several veterans and installing Gehrig, Lazzeri and Koenig full time in the starting lineup. The youngsters all played well. The remaining veterans cut down their after-hours activities and returned to top playing form. Ruth regained his home-run touch. And the Yankees won the pennant.

The St. Louis Cardinals beat the Yanks in the World Series. But this just provided New York with an added incentive for the 1927 season. The Yankees made a mockery of the pennant race. They were in first place every day of the schedule. They dominated every team they faced. Against the hapless St. Louis Browns the Yankees won twenty-one of twenty-two games. After July 1 there was no doubt that they would win the pennant. On that date they met the second-place Washington Senators in a doubleheader.

Washington was riding the crest of a winning streak. The Senators had dreams of sweeping the doubleheader and threatening the Yanks' hold on first place. But Washington's dream soon became

Little Miller Huggins, shown with Manager Bucky Harris of the Senators, masterminded "Murderers' Row."

a nightmare. The Yankees slaughtered the Senators, 12-1, in the first game.

New York, however, was just warming up for the big assault. In the second game the Yanks almost ran Washington out of the league. The final score was 21-1! When the Senators staggered out of Yankee Stadium that night, they were no longer dreaming of the pennant. "Those fellows not only beat you," moaned Washington's first baseman Joe Judge, "they tear your heart out. I wish the season was over."

Nothing could hold the Yankees back, not even an exhausting travel schedule. Once they were supposed to go by train from Boston to Detroit, a very long trip in the 1920s. The train was due to arrive in Detroit about noon, and the game with the Tigers was scheduled to start several hours later. But the train was late. Since many of the Yankees had slept through breakfast, they had to be rushed to the ballpark by a special police escort. They didn't even have time to eat lunch or take batting practice. They just gobbled a few hot dogs and soft drinks, pulled on their uniforms, and went out to meet the well-fed, well-rested Tigers.

New York won the game, 19-2.

The Yankees rallied from behind to win so many times that center fielder Combs began calling their late spurts "Five o'clock Lightening." Because stadiums in those days didn't have lights, all games had to be concluded in daylight. It was usual for the eighth and ninth innings to be played around five o'clock in the afternoon—and this is when the Yankees' blazing comebacks took place. Pitchers throughout the league dreaded the approach of five o'clock and the eighth inning. Against the Yankees no lead, however large, was ever really secure.

The New York team was so popular with fans all around the country that the Yanks played many exhibition games during the regular season. Whenever there was a day off on the schedule the Yanks traveled to St. Paul or Dayton or Buffalo or even to National League cities like Pittsburgh or Cincinnati for exhibition games.

Some players didn't like working on what was supposed to be their day off. But Ruth couldn't have cared less. In spite of his night-time partying, the Babe truly loved to play baseball—even exhibition games. Wherever he played huge crowds assembled. And Babe always responded with a good show. He joked with the fans, he signed countless autographs, and he always tried to hit at least one home run. Once, at an exhibition game in Toronto, Canada, he was actually mobbed on the field by a large crowd of young boys. Some of them leaped on his back, others grabbed him around the legs. Suddenly Babe was buried beneath a squirming mass of adoring youths. Some athletes might have become angry, but Babe thought it was great fun.

"I had the presence of mind to put my cap between by teeth and hold onto it like a dog," Babe said later. "Otherwise one of those little suckers would have stolen it for a souvenir."

Ruth wasn't the only Yankee who liked to enjoy life. New York clinched the pennant in Boston on Labor Day, 1927, almost a month before the season was over. The gruff little Huggins was so delighted he suspended all training rules for the day. "Just make sure you show up at the station at one o'clock in the morning for the train ride back to New York," he announced. "Besides that, I don't care what you do. Have a good time."

The players took Huggins at his word—and had a *very* good time. Several almost missed the train. Their celebration in Boston hadn't been enough, however. They decided to continue on board. The team was supposed to occupy the three cars at the front of the train. But the players boarded from the rear, so they had to pass through all the other cars before they reached their own. As the players walked through the aisles, they noticed that the other passengers had left their shoes in front of their sleeping compartments so the porters could shine them overnight. One of the Yanks thought it might be fun to kick a shoe. Another Yankee tried it. Soon every shoe in the train had been kicked into a large pile. The next morning it took the startled passengers hours to find the proper shoes.

Despite the Yankees' early runaway with the American League pennant, there was one element of suspense during the final month of the season. That excitement was generated by Ruth's great desire to break his own record of fifty-nine home runs. By the final day of the schedule, he had tied the record.

The Yanks' last game was against Washington. A large crowd gathered at the New York stadium to watch Ruth try for number sixty. In his first three times at bat, Ruth had a walk and two singles. But he hit nothing that came close to a home run. In the eighth inning, with the score tied, 2-2, Ruth came up to bat again. This would probably be his last chance unless the game went into extra innings. The pitcher was Tom Zachary, a skillful left-hander with a tricky screwball. Zachary was a very hard man to hit a home run against.

Zachary's first pitch was a screwball that broke sharply over the plate for a called strike. The bat never moved off Babe's shoulder. The crowd groaned. Then Zachary tried his screwball again. The crack of the bat meeting the ball resounded through the Stadium. The fans rose with a yell as the ball headed deep down the right-field foul line. Umpire Bill Dineen crouched on the foul line as the ball landed fifteen rows behind the right-field fence. Everyone in the park held his breath waiting for Dineen to signal whether the ball was fair or foul. Finally Dineen signaled—fair ball.

Ruth had hit his sixtieth home run. The Babe tipped his hat as he rounded the bases. The fans screamed and the Yankee players rushed out of the dugout to meet him at home plate. Now there was just one piece of unfinished business—the World Series. And the Yanks took care of that very quickly.

The Pittsburgh Pirates, New York's opponents, were a good team. But the Pirates were psychologically demoralized before the Series began. The day before the opening game both teams had worked out at Forbes Field in Pittsburgh. The Pirates used the field first. Then they put on their street clothes and sat in the stands to watch the Yanks take batting practice. Huggins knew that the Pittsburgh players had heard frightening tales about the Yankees'

Babe Ruth gets his weight behind a pitch.

power hitters. He also knew that the Pirates had
never seen the Yanks in action. Thus the manager
decided to put on a hitting show for the Pirates'
benefit. Huggins took pitcher Waite Hoyt off to the
side. "You are the starting pitcher tomorrow," he
told Hoyt. "But I want you to pitch a few minutes of
batting practice. Just lay the ball in there nice and
easy."

Hoyt lobbed the ball straight over the plate, and
the Yankees put on an awesome hitting display.

Ruth, Combs, Koenig, Gehrig, Meusel, Lazzeri, Dugan, Collins and Grabowski belted the ball into the stands, over the stands, and out of the ballpark. The Pirate players simply couldn't believe their eyes. Paul "Big Poison" Waner, who weighed only 155 pounds, turned sadly to his brother Lloyd "Little Poison" Waner, a 145-pounder, and sighed. The Waners were Pittsburgh's top hitters, but they had never seen hitting like this. "Gee, they're big," Paul finally said. "And they're so powerful, too." His brother just stared in silence. Finally the Pirates rose slowly and walked out of the park like men in a trance.

But it wasn't the Yankees' power that eventually beat the Pirates. (New York hit just two home runs in the Series.) The Pirates were so jittery after viewing the Yanks' practice slugging that they were never able to play good defense or to mount an effective attack against New York. And the Yankees' pitching was as impressive as it had been all season.

In the opening game, with the score tied 1-1 in the top of the third, the Pirates lost their composure. Koenig's grounder was bobbled for an error. Ruth singled and Gehrig walked to load the bases. Pittsburgh's pitcher, Ray Kremer, then walked Meusel, forcing in the lead run. Next, Lazzeri hit a ground ball that seemed as though it would be turned into an easy doubleplay. But the Pirate infielders muffed it and could do no better than force Meusel at second, while Ruth scored. Then Pittsburgh trapped Gehrig off third base, only to have Pirate catcher "Oil" Smith drop the throw at the plate for another error. Gehrig scored to give the Yankees a 4-1 lead.

In the late innings, Pittsburgh closed the gap to 5-4. But Huggins called in Moore to replace Hoyt, and Wilcy protected the slim lead. In fact, the Yankee pitching was so effective during the remainder of the Series that no other relief help was required.

Huggins started George Pipgras, one of his second line pitchers, in the second game. Pipgras came through with a solid job, and the Yanks won easily, 6-2. New York pounded out eleven hits and Pittsburgh committed two more errors.

By the time the teams moved to New York for the third game, the Yankees were oozing confidence. In a taxicab en route to the stadium, Lazzeri said, "If we don't beat these bums four in a row you can shoot me."

Pennock turned in one of the best pitching performances in Series history that afternoon. Although the Pirates were supposed to do well against left-handed pitchers, they were helpless against Pennock. After the top half of the seventh had been completed, Pennock was pitching a perfect game. Not one Pirate had reached base.

But the Yankee sluggers may have ruined Pennock's chance of becoming the first pitcher to throw a no-hitter in the Series. Leading 2-0, the Yanks suddenly exploded in the last of the seventh. Ruth blasted a three-run homer and by the time the inning came to an end, the Yankees had scored three more runs.

For almost half an hour, Pennock had to sit on the bench as the Yankees galloped around the bases. When he finally returned to the mound, in the top of the eighth, his aging arm had cooled off. He retired the first batter—his twenty-second straight—but then Pittsburgh's star third baseman, Pie Traynor, cracked a single to left field to end Pennock's bid for a perfect game. Two more hits and one run followed. But Pennock still finished with a three-hitter and an 8-1 victory.

The following day the Yanks went out to wrap up the Series. Huggins again surprised many people with his choice of a starting pitcher. This time he selected reliever Wilcy Moore. And once again it turned out to be a good choice. Moore pitched well.

Ruth knocked in Combs with a single in the first inning and belted a long two-run homer in the fifth. But the Pirates fought back, tying the score, 3-3, in the seventh. The game remained deadlocked as the teams moved into the ninth inning.

After Moore had retired Pittsburgh in order in the top of the ninth, the Yankees had their chance to end the Series. The crowd of 57,909 roared for the kill. As usual, the Yankees didn't let their fans down. They put the pressure on Pittsburgh immediately— and the Pirates cracked again.

Combs opened with a walk. Koenig laid down a perfect punt and flashed across first base ahead of Pie Traynor's desperate throw. There were two runners on base with none out. Pittsburgh relief pitcher John Miljus threw a wild pitch and both runners advanced one base. Combs, on third, was just ninety feet away from victory.

Miljus walked Ruth intentionally, loading the bases. Then he struck out Gehrig and Meusel. It seemed that the Pirates might escape. But the dangerous Lazzeri was at the plate. Miljus worked carefully—but maybe too carefully. His pitch was wild and sailed past the catcher. The speedy Combs raced home with the winning run. The Yankees were champions. They had swept the World Series.

1934 St. Louis Cardinals

THE GASHOUSE GANG

America was in the depth of a financial depression in 1934. Millions of men were out of work. Whole families lined up in the streets to receive free food from the government. In addition, a violent revolution in Spain and the rise of a Nazi dictatorship in Germany were disturbing to those Americans who could foresee a future United States involvement. The confident optimism that had typified the 1920s disappeared. Men were having to scrape and struggle for their living.

The 1934 St. Louis Cardinals were a team with which the struggling poor could identify. Unlike the Yankee powerhouse of the 1920s, the Cardinals were an ungraceful bunch who had to fight and scramble for everything they got—including their hits and stolen bases. Many of them had come up from the poverty of the coal mines in the East or the cotton fields and farms of the South. The fans loved them for their hustle on the field, their wild shenanigans off the field and their contempt for authority both on and off the field. The Cardinals treated police and umpires with equal disregard. The times were tough, and the Cardinals acted accordingly.

Leo "The Lip" Durocher, the Cardinals' short-stop, was one of the leaders of the brash team. In fact, it was Leo whose comments gave birth to the nickname, "Gashouse Gang." Early in the 1934 season, a sportswriter asked Leo if the Cards had a chance to win the National League pennant. Before Durocher could answer, he was interrupted by his teammate, Dizzy Dean, the most colorful man among this colorful collection of players. "We could win the pennant in any league," bellowed Dizzy, "American or National."

Durocher, who had played for the incredible New York Yankees during Babe Ruth's era, shook his head. "They wouldn't let us play in the American League. They would say we were just a lot of Gashouse players."

The sportswriter reported Durocher's comments, and from then on the Cardinals were known as the "Gashouse Gang."

The swaggering, hard-nosed ballplayers who formed the 1934 Cardinals were forever achieving the improbable. On September 5 they were seven games out of first place, but before the month was over they had charged ahead to win the pennant. Then they sent the Detroit Tigers swirling to defeat in true Gashouse Gang style in the World Series. To them, nothing was normal; nothing was stable. They were the perfect team for the times of the '30s.

No one exemplified the dizziness of the team more than Jay Hanna "Dizzy" Dean, the team's biggest star. The product of a family of cotton pickers, he emerged from a shack on an Arkansas farm to become the nation's idol at age twenty-three.

With an overpowering fast ball and a sharp breaking curve, he was one of the greatest pitchers of all time. During the 1934 season he was at his best—the last of the thirty-game winners until Denny McLain of Detroit duplicated the feat in 1968.

Dean was a goofy, folksy character, who said and did whatever happened to pop into his head. Once he placed a chunk of ice on home plate before a game. "That's to cool off my fast ball," Dizzy explained. On another occasion, in Boston, he warned the Braves' hitters that he would throw nothing but fast balls. Then he went out to the mound and, true to his word, threw only fast balls— no curves or changeups. Though the Boston hitters knew what pitch was coming, the knowledge did them no good. Dean pitched a three-hitter.

Dizzy's younger brother Paul was also a top Cardinal pitcher. Before the 1934 season started, Dizzy predicted that "Me an' Paul will win forty-five games." For once, Diz underestimated himself. Paul won nineteen, giving the Dean family a total of forty-nine victories.

Twenty-one-year-old Paul was much quieter than Dizzy. But even Paul had his colorful moments. He joined Dizzy in a mid-season strike against the Cardinal management and even suggested that Diz punch the St. Louis manager in the nose. The Deans, however, did not constitute the entire 1934 Cardinal pitching staff. Tex Carleton, a strong right-hander, who went on to win more than a hundred big league games, won sixteen that season. Bill Walker, a veteran lefty, finished with a 12-4 record.

The Dean brothers—Daffy, left, and Dizzy, right—were forever clowning around on the field.

The Cardinals' fighting spirit was typified by their player-manager Frankie Frisch, who played second base. Frisch was a graduate of Fordham University, where he had earned the nickname "The Fordham Flash." But he really learned his brand of fiery baseball under tough old John McGraw, who was still managing the New York Giants when Frisch played for the team in the 1920s. By 1934 "The Flash," who was in his first season as player-manager of the Cardinals, was beginning to age. But Frankie had lost none of his competitive fire. And he could still handle a bat. Frisch hit .305 in 140 games.

Rip Collins, the Cardinals' first baseman, topped

the National League in home runs with thirty-five.
He also led the league in practical jokes. He specialized in dropping water bombs from hotel windows.
Once, when he was to speak at an important ban-
quet, Collins arrived early and sprinkled sneezing
powder around the room. The guests sneezed so
much they could hardly hear Rip's speech.

Durocher, the shortstop, was a confident, aggressive player, who later became a famous manager.
While with the Yankees, he had actually had the
nerve to punch Babe Ruth in the nose. Although a
slick fielder, Leo's hitting was weak. Ruth used to
call him "the All-American out." In 1934, however,
Leo hit a respectable .260.

All the Cardinals loved to argue with umpires.
But Durocher and Frisch were so caustic in their
comments that some umpires retaliated by giving
opponents the benefit of the doubt on close plays.

Third baseman Pepper Martin was known as
"The Wild Horse of the Osage," after the section of
Oklahoma from which he came. Martin was a
rugged fellow with a bull neck, wide shoulders,
powerful arms and gnarled hands. In his youth, he
had worked on farms, dug holes for telephone
poles and herded horses and cattle. By compari-
son with his boyhood labors, baseball seemed easy
work. Martin, who broke into the big leagues as an
outfielder, knocked down ground balls with his
chest and slid into bases on his stomach. His trade-
mark was the dirty uniform. In the 1931 World
Series he had beaten the Philadelphia Athletics almost single-handedly with a .500 batting average
and five stolen bases.

Pepper loved to dress like a gangster. Once he walked into a boarding house with a shotgun and several hunting dogs, and registered as "Pretty Boy Floyd," one of the most notorious criminals of that era. A few minutes later, a sheriff's posse arrived. They had come to put "Pretty Boy Floyd" in jail. Pepper had to do some fast talking to convince them who he really was—and wasn't.

During the 1934 season, Martin hit .289 and led the league in stolen bases. One day when the team was short-handed, he even pitched two innings as a relief pitcher. But Pepper caused Frisch plenty of

Pepper Martin's daring on the basepaths has been matched by few. Here he scores against the Tigers.

headaches, too. One day he arrived late at the park. He was covered with grease.

"Where have you been?" screamed Frisch.

"I bet a guy I could beat him in a two-mile midget-car race," Martin explained seriously, "and he was late showing up."

"That's great," the manager moaned. "We're trying to win the pennant and you're trying to win a bet! How much was the bet?"

"Two quarts of ice cream," Martin answered. Meanwhile, his face began to turn a sickly color.

"What's the matter?" asked Frisch.

"I ate both quarts," Pepper admitted.

Frisch turned away, shaking his head hopelessly. "We're not crazy. We're perfectly sane," he mumbled.

Joe Medwick, the left fielder, was one of the game's best hitters. His lifetime batting average of .324 has since earned him a place in the Hall of Fame. In 1934 Medwick hit .319 and led the league with eighteen triples. Medwick had a terrible temper and he was never a man to shy away from a fight. One day, for instance, Dizzy Dean was pitching with a very big lead and began to fool around. He lazily lobbed the ball over the plate and some long drives resulted. Soon Medwick got tired of chasing the ball in left field.

When the inning was over, Dizzy sat down next to Medwick in the dugout. "If you are anywhere near me five seconds from now, I'm going to kill you," Medwick snarled. Dean didn't wait to find out if Joe was serious. He got away as fast as possible.

But on another occasion, when Dizzy had gotten

into a fight with a sportswriter and a second writer took a swing at Dean, Medwick knocked the second writer out cold with one punch.

Center fielder Ernie Orsatti was so agile that he worked as a stuntman in Hollywood movies during the off-season. His teammates called him "Showboat" because of his fancy catches.

Right fielder Jack Rothrock was the least known of the Gashouse Gang. But he was one of the most dependable. In 1934, Rothrock hit .284 and was the only Cardinal who played in every game.

St. Louis also had strength behind the plate. In fact, Frisch had his choice of two fine catchers. In the early part of the season he relied on slow-footed Virgil "Spud" Davis, who finished the year with a .300 batting average. But, by the time the pennant race was in the home stretch, the Cards' catching was in the hands of young Bill DeLancey. Just twenty-two years old, Bill hit .316 that season and seemed to be headed for stardom. DeLancey, however, was a man fated for tragedy. In 1940 he had to retire because of his health, and by 1946 he had died of tuberculosis.

Branch Rickey, the man who put the Gashouse Gang together, was a complete contrast to his high-living crew. As the Cardinals' general manager, he was one of the shrewdest front-office men in baseball. His trades had brought men like Frisch and Durocher to St. Louis. More important, he was the first man to develop a far-reaching minor league system. From the Cards' farm teams had come the Deans, DeLancey, Collins, Martin, Orsatti and Medwick.

Rickey was a serious, religious man who never drank. Apparently his standards didn't always rub off on his team. The Cards were a reckless, boisterous group. In 1933 they had finished in fifth place and didn't seem to let their poor showing bother them. The New York Giants won the championship and were favored to repeat in 1934.

The Cardinals began the 1934 season poorly, losing seven of their first eleven games. Frisch was furious. He knew he had to do something to shake up the team. He called a meeting, locked the clubhouse door and laid down the law. "If you'd rather go back to the mines and dig coal than ride around the country in Pullmans and live in the best hotels at the club's expense, speak right up," he shouted. "We haven't any room for softies, and no holds are barred. That's the way we're going to play ball."

For a moment the team sat in silence. Then Dean shouted, "You said more'n a mouthful, Dutchman." The rest of the players roared their agreement. From that day on the Cardinals were locked in a three-way fight for the pennant with the Giants and the Chicago Cubs.

Nevertheless, the Gashouse Gang still had plenty of time for fun. During fielding practice, 165-pound Pepper Martin would exhibit his strength by carrying 180-pound Rip Collins piggyback around the outfield while catching fungos at the same time.

On road trips, water bombs and sneezing powder were everywhere. But occasionally one of the pranks backfired. For instance, one day Martin arrived for a game in Boston with his thumb heavily bandaged. Frisch didn't notice the injury until Pepper made his first throw. As the third baseman released the ball, the bandage unraveled and blood squirted from a deep cut. Frisch rushed over from second base.

"Get out of here," he said to Martin. "You can't play with that. You may need stitches."

But Martin, toughened by the cattle country where he grew up, wanted to stay in the game. "I can play," he pleaded. "Just give me a hand with this bandage."

"Beat it," Frisch yelled.

Pepper left the field. Later, Frisch discovered how Pepper had injured his hand. In the Cardinals' hotel there were several well-dressed elderly ladies who walked their dogs every night at ten o'clock. Martin, who couldn't resist a prank, had filled a pitcher with water and poured it over the women and animals when they walked past his window. But he had laughed so hard that he slammed the pitcher against the window sill. The pitcher had broken and cut Martin's hand.

"A very nice story," Frisch moaned when he heard the tale. "A big league ballplayer throwing water on old ladies and their dogs. And he cuts his thumb and can't play ball. I may have a heart attack before this season is over!"

Dizzy Dean enjoyed needling the hot tempered manager, too, especially during the most serious moments at clubhouse meetings. The meetings bored Dizzy and he sought ways to break them up. Martin and Collins were always willing to help. Once, when Frisch was trying to explain a complex cut-off play, Dean gave a huge yawn and whispered to Martin, "Let's get this thing over with."

Frisch, deep in thought, paused to ask if the players had any questions about what he had just explained.

"May I speak?" Martin asked. Frisch smiled. It pleased him to think that Pepper was concentrating his interest in the technical side of baseball. Martin shuffled to the front of the room and pulled a rumpled piece of paper from his back pocket. "Here's something that puzzled me, Frank," he said very earnestly. "The man at the garage soaked me thirty-four dollars to fix my midget auto racer. I think this bill is much too high."

Frisch's eyes widened in disbelief. Dean, aware that the manager was totally confused, nodded to Collins to join in the hoax. "I don't think it's too high, Frank," said Collins.

"It's robbery," yelled Dizzy. "What did he fix?"

"Well," said Martin. "He fixed a valve intake in the engine and . . ." By now all the players had caught on to the joke. Everyone was shouting his opinion of Pepper's garage bill. The clubhouse was in turmoil.

"What does Martin's racer have to do with a ball game?" screamed Frisch. "Why you guys— All right, meeting dismissed!"

As if that wasn't enough to drive Frisch nutty, the Dean brothers decided to go on strike in August while the Cards were in the midst of the pennant race.

The team had just lost a double-header to the Cubs. Both Dizzy and Paul had been knocked out of the box, so they were already in a sour mood when they learned that the Cardinals' owner, Sam Breadon, had scheduled an exhibition game in Detroit for the next day. This meant that the Cards would not get a day off. The Dean brothers decided not to go to Detroit. When the Cardinals' train headed toward Michigan, the Deans were not aboard. Breadon fined Dizzy $100 and Paul $50. The two players refused to pay the fines and were suspended. Furthermore, Dizzy summoned a group of photographers and publicly tore up two Cardinal uniforms. The club fined him $36 for damages. "That's not nice," Dizzy said. "They could'a been mended."

While the Cardinals continued to play, Dizzy sat in the stands in St. Louis and loudly predicted, "Frisch won't win the pennant without us."

But the Cards promptly won seven of their next eight games. The Deans got the message. Paul and Dizzy quietly abandoned their strike.

Even with the Deans, St. Louis lagged behind the Giants. On September 5, the Cardinals were still tied with the Cubs for second place and were seven games behind the first-place Giants. Time was running out. Then the Gashouse Gang began its big push. By September 13, when they came into New York for a four-game series, they had cut the lead to five and a half games. Paul Dean pitched a shutout in the opener, winning 2-0 in twelve innings. The Giants won the second game, 4-1. Frisch knew he had to sweep the double-header the following day, so he started the Dean brothers, even though Paul had had just one day of rest.

There wasn't an empty seat in the Polo Grounds when the game began. Dizzy pitched against New York's ace, "King" Carl Hubbell. Often, during the game, Durocher asked for the ball so that he could rub it up for Dizzy. Actually, the wily Leo was scratching up the ball illegally with his roughened belt buckle so that each pitch Dizzy threw had a little extra "stuff" on it. Dizzy really didn't need the help, though. He was good enough to win on his own. The Cards took the first game, 5-3.

Paul Dean was brilliant in the second game. He kept the Giants handcuffed until the eleventh inning. Then, with the score tied 1-1, Pepper Martin belted a home run. The Cards won, 3-1. Now New York was leading by just three and a half games.

But the Giants refused to fold. As a result the Cardinals hadn't moved up much closer by the time they entered Ebbets Field on September 21 for a double-header with the Dodgers. Dizzy and Paul were scheduled to pitch. Frisch called a clubhouse meeting to discuss the Brooklyn hitters. Most of the players were tense. But not Dizzy.

"Keep the ball high and outside to Leslie," Frisch warned his pitchers during the meeting. "He'll hit it over the fence if you don't."

"Ain't how I pitch him," Dean interrupted. "I give him low and inside stuff and he ain't got a hit off me yet."

Frisch tried to ignore his heckling pitcher. "Nothing but curve balls to Tony," he said. "This guy murders the fastball."

"Funny thing," Dizzy piped up. "I haven't dished him a curve ball yet and he's still tryin' to get his first loud foul off ol' Diz."

Frisch got madder and madder. Finally Dean announced, "What a silly business this is, Frankie. I've already won twenty-six games and it don't look right for an infielder like you to be tellin' a star like me how to pitch."

The manager blew his stack. "You can pitch as you damn please," Frisch screamed. "You meathead. I hope the Dodgers pin your ears back."

"They ain't pinning ol' Diz's ears back none," Dizzy answered with a laugh. "I doubt if them Dodgers even get a hit off me an' Paul. We're gonna be one-hit Dean and no-hit Dean today."

Unbelievably, Dizzy was almost 100 per cent accurate. Diz pitched a three-hitter to win the opener. Paul pitched a no-hitter in the second game. "If you'da told me you wuz gonna pitch a no-hitter," Dizzy drawled to his brother after the game, "I'da bore down instead of just coastin' and I'da pitched me a no-hitter, too." Frisch was speechless—but very happy.

The Cards traveled to Chicago. Hordes of writers had been sent there from all over the country to cover the sizzling pennant race. And everyone wanted to interview Dizzy. One afternoon Dean granted each newsman an "exclusive" interview, one at a time. His friend, St. Louis sportswriter Roy Stockton, acted as traffic manager and also sat in on each interview. By the end of the day Stockton was flabbergasted. "How could you do a thing like that?" he asked Diz.

"Like what?" Dizzy replied.

"You gave each writer a *different* answer to the *same* question!" said Stockton.

"Why, Roy," explained Dean, "you didn't expect

Dizzy Dean could pitch as well as he wanted to.

me to give 'em all the same story did you? They all come from different papers. If they went back with the same story, their editors wouldn't like it and maybe the fellers would be in trouble."

The writers, however, weren't exactly grateful the next day when they discovered that each man had an embarrassingly different version of what Dizzy had to say.

But by that time Dizzy's mind was elsewhere. He beat Pittsburgh, 3-2, on September 25, scoring his twenty-eighth victory. The Giants lost to Philadelphia so St. Louis trailed by just one game. Three days later Dizzy shut out the Cincinnati Reds, 4-0, moving the Cards into a tie for first place. There were just two games to go.

The Giants still had to play the hapless Brooklyn Dodgers, but they expected those games to be a cinch. Earlier in the season, however, New York's playing-manager, Bill Terry, had made a careless remark about the Brooklyn team that was about to come back to haunt him. Sprotswriters had asked Terry in April if he expected Brooklyn to have a good team. The Giants' boss had cracked: "Brooklyn? Is Brooklyn still in the league?"

Though the Dodgers did have a pretty poor club, they had vowed that they would make Terry pay for his wisecrack. Now they had their chance. With the boisterous Brooklyn fans cheering them on, they invaded the Polo Grounds and clobbered the Giants, 5-1.

Meanwhile, in Cincinnati, Paul Dean beat the Reds, 6-1. The Cardinals had clinched a tie for the pennant. But they were not interested in ties. Frisch sent Dizzy back to the mound on the final day of the season. Although it was Dean's third start in six days, he wasn't even tired. He pitched another shut-out. The Cardinals won, 9-0. And Brooklyn beat the Giants again.

The Gashouse Gang had won the pennant!

The Cardinals' opponents in the World Series were the Detroit Tigers. Detroit had a rugged, long-ball-hitting lineup and a deep pitching staff. The Tigers were expected to give St. Louis trouble. But Dizzy wasn't concerned. "I think I'd like to pitch every game," he proclaimed.

"You can't win four straight," said an astonished listener.

"Maybe not." Dizzy laughed. "But I sure can win four out-ta five."

Dizzy had pitched two shutouts in the final three games of the season, a feat that would make most pitchers plead for a rest. But Diz was delighted when Frisch named him to start the opening game of the Series. Though he had had just two days' rest, the Tigers were no match for him. Before the game had even started, Dizzy began unsettling his oppo-nents. During batting practice he stuck his head into the Tigers' dugout and said to Detroit's leading home-run hitter, Hank Greenberg, "How come you're so white? You're a-shakin' like a leaf."

Dean, still in his street clothes, shuffled over to the batting cage where fiery Mickey Cochrane, the Tigers' great catcher and playing-manager, was at the plate. Dizzy brazenly grabbed the bat from Cochrane's hands, took his stance against the bat-ting-practice pitcher, and hit the first pitch into the stands. The Tigers' mouths dropped open. "Mick," said Dizzy sympathetically, "I'm the worst hitter we have."

Each member of the Tiger infield committed an error that day, and Dean handcuffed the Tiger batters. St. Louis won the opener, 8-3. In the clubhouse Dean spoke over a shortwave radio to explorer Admiral Richard Byrd, who was in Antarctica. "Howdy, Dick Byrd," drawled Diz. "I could-a brought four teams from the National League over here and won the American League pennant."

The Tigers were no pushovers, though. In the second game, "Schoolboy" Rowe, their best pitcher, retired the last twenty-two Cardinals and Detroit won, 3-2 in twelve innings. The Series then shifted to St. Louis, where Paul Dean pitched the Cards to a 4-1 victory.

Detroit pulled even by winning the fourth game, 10-4. Yet Dizzy managed to remain the major topic of conversation. In the fourth inning the Cardinals started a rally. Frisch sent Dean, who was an excellent all-round athlete, to first base as a pinch runner. Martin bounced the ball to the second baseman, who flipped to the shortstop to force Dean. The shortstop then fired to first to complete the double play. But the ball never reached first base. Maybe Dean was trying to break up the double play. Maybe he just forgot to slide. At any rate, the throw smacked him in the forehead and Dean went down as though he had been shot by a rifle. He was carried off the field and taken to the hospital for X-rays.

After the game, Paul Dean spoke to newsmen.

"He's fine," said Paul. "He weren't unconscious at all. He talked all the way to the clubhouse."

"What was he saying?" asked a reporter.

"Oh, he weren't sayin' nothin'," explained Paul. "Diz was just talkin'."

Dizzy returned the next day. His head hurt but he announced that he would still pitch the fifth game of the Series that afternoon. "They X-rayed my head and found nothin'," Dizzy noted. "I saw stars, moons and all sorts of animals, but no Tigers."

Although Dean pitched well, the Tigers won, 3-1. Now the Gashouse Gang was in trouble. The last two games of the Series were to be played in Detroit. One defeat for St. Louis and it was all over. But the Cards bristled with defiance. "We haven't cracked yet," shouted Durocher.

"We got it in the bag," said Pepper Martin.

Paul Dean started for the Cardinals in the sixth game. In the seventh inning, with the score tied, 3-3, Paul singled. Durocher then smacked his third hit, a booming double. Dean scored the lead run. St. Louis hung on to win, 4-3. There was pandemonium in the Cards' clubhouse. Dizzy hugged Paul and shouted, "You're the greatest pitcher the Dean family ever had." Diz had purchased a rubber Tiger, a souvenir sold to the Detroit fans, and he raced around the clubhouse swinging it over his head. Then he threw it into the showers at Pepper Martin.

At first, Frisch pretended that he was going to use Bill Hallahan as his starting pitcher in the seventh game. Dizzy, for once the butt of someone else's joke, howled: "You can't pitch him. You gotta pitch ol' Diz. I'm the only one sure to win."

Durocher kept the Tigers on edge in the sixth game of the Series.

But later that night Frisch admitted to Dean that he had just been kidding. "Diz," he said. "Do you want to be the greatest man in baseball?"

"I already am," Dizzy replied.

"You're going to start tomorrow," Frisch continued. "If you win you'll be tops."

"Look, Frankie," said Dean. "Just gimme that ball tomorrow and your troubles will be over."

The next day Dean stood nearby as Detroit's starter, a pitcher named Eldon Auker, warmed up. Then Diz walked over to Cochrane and told the Detroit manager, "He just won't do, Mickey. He just won't do."

Auker didn't do. The rambunctious Cardinal hitters jumped all over him. In the third, Dizzy singled. Then Martin hit a slow roller to the infield. "The Wild Horse of the Osage" grimaced, churned his spikes and beat the throw to first base for a hit. Auker next walked Rothrock to fill the bases. Then Frankie Frisch came to bat. The playing manager had a chance to win the game—and the Series—for his team, and he made the most of it. Frisch slashed a double, sending three runs across the plate. "I couldn't let the rest of them make an old man out of me," he said later.

The Tigers were desperate. From the bullpen came Detroit's best pitcher, "Schoolboy" Rowe. But Rip Collins greeted him with a double. DeLancey followed with another double. Rowe headed for the showers. Before Detroit could get its third out, Dean had beaten out an infield grounder (his second hit of the inning) and St. Louis had gone on to score seven runs.

As the Cards' lead mounted, the Tigers and their fans became increasingly angry and frustrated. In the sixth inning, Medwick slid hard into third base- man Marv Owen after hitting a triple. Medwick was convinced that Owen had tried to stomp on him with his spikes. The St. Louis slugger kicked Owen in the chest. Suddenly Medwick and Owen were trading punches. The umpires had to drag them apart.

When Medwick went to left field in the last of the sixth, the furious Detroit fans bombarded him with everything they could get their hands on. Pop bot- tles, scorecards and fruit sailed out of the bleach- ers. The umpires called time out and the debris was cleared away. But when Medwick returned to his

position, the barrage began again. The home plate
umpire asked Frisch to take Medwick out of the
game. St. Louis was leading, 9-0, but Medwick had
hit .379 during the Series and Frisch—who never
gave his opponents an inch—refused to send in a
substitute. Four times Medwick tried to reach left
field. Each time he was driven back. Finally, Judge
Kenesaw Mountain Landis, the commissioner of
baseball, summoned Medwick and Owen to his box.
The players refused to shake hands.

"Did you kick him?" Landis asked Medwick.

"You're darn right I did!" shouted Medwick.

"You are out of the game," Landis said. His decision prevented a riot. But even a riot couldn't have
saved the Tigers. The Cards had a 9-0 lead and
Dean's pitching was almost flawless.

In the last of the ninth, with St. Louis leading
11-0, Frisch refused to take any chances. He sent
four pitchers down to the bullpen to get ready in
case Dean faltered. Dizzy just chuckled. He was
having a good time and he intended to continue
having a good time. With one out and two runners
on base, Diz faced Greenberg, Detroit's best hitter.
"What!" Dean yelled to the Tiger bench. "No pinch
hitter? I already struck this guy out twice."

Dean threw two fastballs past Greenberg. When
the slugger swung and missed the second of them,
Dizzy began laughing so hard he had to put his
glove over his face. Frisch raced to the mound. "We
are two outs away from winning the World Series,"
he stormed, "and you are fooling around. Cut it
out!"

Durocher trotted over. Leo was grinning. "Aw,

Frank, let the guy have his fun. What's the matter with you?"

Frisch just got angrier. "You lose this guy," he warned Dean, "and you are coming out of the ballgame." Dizzy just shrugged his shoulders. Then he threw his fastball. As it hurtled toward home plate, Dean actually turned his back on the batter. Greenberg swung and missed. Moments later Dean had his shutout and the World Series was over.

In the clubhouse later there was a wild celebration. Dizzy waved his rubber Tiger and sang his favorite country songs. Then Frisch walked over to Dean and snapped, "Anybody with your stuff should have won forty games this year instead of a measly thirty. You loaf, that's your trouble. You ought to be ashamed of yourself."

But the Gashouse Gang just broke into laughter. Even Frisch had to smile.

1948 Cleveland Indians

FIREWORKS IN CLEVELAND

Big league baseball seemed the ideal investment for Bill Veeck when he purchased the Cleveland Indians in 1946. Soldiers and sailors were back from World War II, and there were few things they wanted more than some real live entertainment, American style. Baseball provided the perfect answer. Television had not yet taken its grip on the country, and professional football was still playing second fiddle to the college game. Moreover, Veeck was a master showman, the very kind of host that baseball needed.

But Cleveland hardly seemed the perfect situation, even for a promoter like Veeck. The team was one of the worst franchises in baseball. Not since 1920 had the Indians won a pennant. Rarely were they even close to the top. The fans responded to such dull play by staying away from the ballpark. At a time when most teams had surpassed the million mark in home attendance, the Indians had yet to come close to such a record.

But Veeck was undaunted. At least Cleveland was a major league franchise, and he figured that was

*Showboating owner Bill Veeck, right, provides his manager,
Lou Boudreau, with a giant bottle of aspirins.*

the first step required to put his own talents to work.
Veeck barged into the seemingly hopeless situation
as if he had just bought the New York Yankees.

With equal zest, he went about the dual tasks of
building a team and building up the gate. Within
two years' time, his once shabby franchise had become the best in baseball—in both respects.

A daring maverick, Bill scandalized the conserva-
tive club owners and league officials with his zany
promotions. He put on fireworks displays before
games, gave free gifts to the fans and even set up a
baby-sitting service at the ballpark. Other owners
howled with anger when Bill signed Larry Doby,
the first black player in the American League. They
called Veeck a "bush-leaguer" when he presented a

fan with an outhouse at home plate. But it took only two years for Veeck to have the last laugh. The Cleveland Indians won the 1948 pennant and set a major league attendance record (2,620,627) that has never been topped.

From the start, Veeck had two major problems: apathetic fans and inept ballplayers. He spruced up the ballpark, fixed the rest rooms, improved the refreshments and added extra ticket windows so fans could reduce their waiting time in line. Veeck wanted the people of Cleveland to be comfortable at Municipal Stadium, and if they couldn't get to the game, he wanted them to be in touch with the Indians. Thus he saw to it that all games, either at home or away, were broadcast on the radio.

Many of Veeck's critics called him a clown who sullied the dignity of the game. But, in truth, his circus acts and fireworks didn't detract from the quality of baseball he maintained. Instead, the additional entertainment helped keep the fans interested and excited when there was no action to watch on the playing field. Veeck wanted every minute of the fans' trip to the ballpark to be enjoyable. His philosophy was simple: "Every day is Mardi Gras and every fan is a king."

"We showed the fans that we weren't just out for their money," Veeck wrote in his autobiography, *Veeck—As In Wreck,* "that we cared about them and wanted them to have a good time."

Veeck hired two baseball comedians, Max Patkin and Jackie Price, to perform at home games. Both were former ballplayers. Patkin often coached first base for a few innings. Sometimes, when he didn't like an umpire's decision, he would topple over on his back like a falling tree. The fans loved him. And they loved Price, too. Jackie could play catch while standing on his head and hit a pitched ball while hanging by his knees from a portable trapeze. He could stand at home plate and throw one ball to the mound and another ball to second base all in the same motion. But the strangest thing about Price was his love of live snakes. He often wore a snake around his waist like a belt.

Veeck had special nights for everybody and everything. There were nights for ladies, "A" students, cab drivers, bartenders, and Boy Scouts. Veeck gave away silk stockings and orchids to women. He set up a nursery with a dozen attendants so parents could bring small children to the game. Before one game he held a cow-milking contest on the field among the Cleveland players. On the final day of the season he opened up the gates and let everyone in free.

Veeck knew what the fans wanted because he wandered through the stands during the games to find out. He sat among the paying customers and chatted with them. The experience taught him one fact: despite all his crazy stunts and concern for the fans' comfort, he could never sell a losing team to the people of Cleveland. So Veeck set out to build a winner.

Upon taking over the team in 1946, Veeck inherited just two legitimate stars. One was Bob Feller, the greatest right-handed pitcher of his day and one of the greatest ever to play the game. The Iowa farm boy had set the major leagues ablaze with his amazing fast ball in 1936 while he was still in his teens. "Rapid Robert" was his nickname and he set all kinds of strikeout records. When he added an excellent curve to his fast ball, he became almost unbeatable.

Feller missed four baseball seasons at the prime of his career because, like most top players of that time, he was in the Armed Forces during World War II. But he came back from the war in 1946 and struck out 348 batters that season to set a record which still stands. Feller went on to win 266 major-league games.

Boudreau was nicknamed "the Boy Manager." But he was a real man when he batted and played shortstop in the 1940s.

Lou Boudreau was Veeck's other star and Cleveland's most popular player. A former basketball star at the University of Illinois, Boudreau became a slick fielding shortstop, who used his great knowledge of the hitters to compensate for his lack of speed. He also was a fine hitter. Boudreau was the Indians' playing manager. He had held this position since 1942 when, at the age of twenty-four, he had volunteered for the job. In 1948 people were still calling him "The Boy Manager."

Veeck was a daring trader. To give Boudreau some good material to work with, Veeck began dealing players left and right. "We've got three teams," Bill joked. "One here, one coming and one going."

His first major trade came after the 1946 season in which the Indians had finished in sixth place. The deal was probably his finest. Veeck traded Allie Reynolds, a very good pitcher, to the New York Yankees for three players. The three players—Joe Gordon, Hal Peck and Gene Bearden—helped Veeck and Cleveland win the pennant.

The most important player in the trade was Joe Gordon, an aging All-Star who had suffered through a poor season in 1946. Some people thought Gordon was finished. But Veeck was convinced Joe still had several good years left. Veeck was correct. Gordon combined with Boudreau to form the best double-play combination in the league. "He's such a great fielder," Boudreau said, "that I sometimes get so interested watching Gordon make one of those patented plays of his I forget I'm in the ballgame too. I act just like a spectator."

The Indian players quickly learned to respect Gordon's maturity and determination. He became the team leader. And, in the pennant year of 1948, he had his best season with thirty-two home runs and 124 runs batted in.

Peck and Bearden were supposedly unimportant minor leaguers. Peck had played for Veeck when Bill owned a minor league team in Milwaukee. Veeck considered Peck, an outfielder, his good-luck charm. In 1948, Peck was more than that. He suddenly blossomed into a fine clutch hitter.

Bearden, who had been a throw-in in the trade, was the biggest surprise. Veeck had wanted a pitcher, and the Yankees gave him a choice of several obscure minor leaguers. Veeck chose Bearden. He took the handsome knuckle baller on the advice of Casey Stengel, who was then the manager of the Oakland team in the Pacific Coast League. "If the Yankees are crazy enough to give him up," Case said, "grab him."

In 1948 Bearden reached the majors and became a star. He won twenty games for the Indians and was voted the Rookie of the Year award. The next season, however, when Stengel became the manager of the New York Yankees, he spread the word around the American League that Bearden's feared knuckle ball actually wasn't in the strike zone very often. Batters stopped swinging at the pitch, and umpires called it a ball. Bearden had to resort to his weak fastball and curveball. He was never a star again. But in 1948, before Stengel exposed his knuckle ball, Bearden was a sensation.

Just before the 1948 season began, Veeck decided

that he needed a good relief pitcher. His choice was startling. Veeck paid the Philadelphia Athletics $25,000 for Russ Christopher, a frail-looking fellow with a baffling pitching motion. Christopher threw almost underhand, like a softball pitcher. His pitch had a sinking trajectory that forced batters to hit the ball into the dirt. This made him the perfect pitcher when a quick double play was needed.

The deal for Christopher was particularly surprising because no one had thought the forty-year-old reliever would ever play again. Because of a weak heart, the pitcher lacked stamina. To make matters much worse, he had contracted pneumonia during spring training in 1948. Nevertheless, the Indians' owner knew that Christopher loved baseball more than anything else. "If I die," Russ had once said, "let me die pitching." Veeck decided to take a chance on him.

Bill approached Connie Mack, the owner and manager of the Athletics, while Christopher was still in the hospital at spring training. "I'll give you $25,000 for him if I can talk to him first," Veeck said to Mack.

"He's a sick man," Mack cautioned. "He can't play."

"That's not your problem," said Veeck. Then he entered Christopher's room and said, "Hey Russ, do you think you can pitch?"

"I don't know," replied Christopher, who was too weak to speak above a whisper.

"Do you want to?" Veeck asked.

"Sure I want to," said Russ. "I'm a pitcher and I want to pitch. But I don't know. . . ."

"I'm going to go down and buy your contract," Veeck told him. "I'll gamble on you."

"Bill," said the grateful Christopher, "I think you're crazy, but you have my word on one thing: I'll give you the best I can."

Veeck's gamble paid off. Christopher pitched, and he pitched well. He didn't have the strength to throw more than a few warm-up pitches in the bullpen, and often he was used for only an inning or even a single batter. But he won three games and saved over a dozen more. In four different games he threw just one pitch. Each time the batter hit into a double play.

Veeck also developed some fine players on his own. Bob Lemon, a weak-hitting third baseman, had been converted into a pitcher in 1946. By 1948

In Veeck's shuffling of players, third baseman Bob Lemon became a pitcher—and a consistent twenty-game winner.

the good-natured, hard-throwing Lemon, with a 20-14 record, was a mainstay of the Cleveland pitching staff.

From the minors came catcher Jim Hegan, a light hitter but an excellent defensive catcher who always knew what pitch to tell the pitchers to throw. Also from the minors came big first baseman Eddie Robinson, who hit fourteen home runs in 1948, and Dale Mitchell, an outfielder who always got his bat on the ball. In 1948 he batted .336 and ran up a twenty-one game hitting streak.

One of Veeck's most meaningful additions to the team was center fielder Larry Doby, the first black player in the American League. Jackie Robinson had joined the Brooklyn Dodgers during spring training of 1947, breaking the major league color barrier. But the American League continued its traditional policy of racial discrimination. There were no black players in the league. Veeck, however, had his own plan.

He signed Doby, a young second baseman who played in the Negro National League—one of the leagues in which black athletes were forced to play because they were barred from organized baseball. Veeck believed that Doby was the best young black player in the country. He signed Larry on July 3, 1947, and Doby immediately joined the Indians.

Doby had a rough year in 1947. He was a sensitive 22-year-old, who came from Paterson, New Jersey. He had never before encountered the resentment and discrimination that he faced that first season in the majors. Many owners of other American League teams publicly blasted Veeck for signing a black man. They said it was just another of Veeck's publicity stunts. Many opposing players, especially those from the South, were furious. Even some of Doby's Cleveland teammates were unfriendly to the frightened rookie.

Doby wasn't prepared for the insults that flew from many opposing dugouts, the pitches that knocked him down, and the second baseman who actually spit tobacco juice in Larry's face as he slid into the bag. Lonely and confused, Doby played poorly in his first season and the fans in many cities booed him loudly.

But in spring training before the 1948 season, Larry was converted into a center fielder. His play began to improve. Still, it was a tough spring for him. He wasn't allowed to live with his teammates in the Indians' hotel headquarters in Tucson, Arizona. Black people were not allowed in the hotel. "The worst thing," Larry recalls, "was not having anyone to communicate with. I was all alone."

Nevertheless, Doby's confidence increased with each game. By the time the season started, it was clear that he was headed for stardom. In the first month of the pennant race, Doby hit a 450-foot home run in Washington—the longest hit in Griffith Stadium up to that time. He went on to hit .301 with fourteen home runs in 1948.

Veeck's concern for his men as human beings, not just as ballplayers, paid off again with third baseman Ken Keltner. The husky slugger seemed near the end of his career in 1946. Yet in 1947 Veeck promised him a $5,000 bonus if he had a good season. Keltner played well that year, but throughout

Because Veeck was willing to take a chance, Larry Doby became the first Negro to play in the American League.

the season his line drives seemed to go straight to opposing fielders. His luck was all bad. Although he hit the ball hard, his batting average was just .257. But on the last day of the season Veeck called Keltner to his office. "I've got $5,000 for you," Veeck said. Keltner was stunned.

"I didn't earn it, Bill," he stammered. "I didn't have a good average." Then Keltner began to cry with gratitude.

"You hit the ball better than anyone else on this club," Veeck said. "It wasn't your fault they kept catching it. You deserve the money."

Keltner repaid Veeck by giving him a great season in 1948. Ken had usually been quite casual about his training habits. But the winter before the 1948 season he worked hard getting into top condition. When spring training opened, he was ready and eager to go. At the age of thirty-one he had one of his best years with thirty-one home runs and a .297 batting average.

Veeck made several other trades which strengthened the Indians. From the Yankees, he brought outfielder Allie Clark. An ironworker in the off-season, Clark was exceptionally strong. He could also handle a bat. Clark hit .310 in 1948.

Early in the season, because Veeck was desperate for a reliable left-handed pitcher to round out his staff, he gave the St. Louis Browns $100,000 for Sam Zoldak, a pitcher who would never have been worth that much under normal circumstances.

Zoldak let the price tag go to his head just a little. He would sit in the Cleveland clubhouse and ask his teammates, "They paid $100,000 for me, how much are *you* worth?" Actually, though, Zoldak was a valuable addition. He was used both as a starter and as a reliever and he compiled a 9-6 record.

But perhaps the best thing that happened to the 1948 Indians was a trade Veeck *didn't* make. The owner had never been very impressed with Boudreau's ability as a manager. In fact, he had repeatedly tried to convince Lou to give up his managing job and just play shortstop. When Bill realized that Boudreau would not step down, he decided to trade him. During the 1947 World Series, Veeck met with St. Louis Browns officials and agreed to give up his playing-manager in a multi-player deal. Veeck planned to name Casey Stengel as the Indians' new manager.

But when the story appeared in the Cleveland newspapers, the fans were furious. Veeck may not have liked Boudreau as a manager, but the fans loved him. Until then, they had also liked Veeck, but now they were ready to lynch him. One newspaper published a "Boudreau Ballot," asking its readers to express their opinions on the proposed trade. Ninety per cent were against it. One man sent the following telegram to Veeck in New York: IF BOUDREAU DOESN'T RETURN TO CLEVELAND, DON'T YOU BOTHER TO RETURN EITHER. Veeck was in danger of losing all the good will he had built up with the Cleveland fans.

Suddenly the Browns withdrew from the deal. Later they traded Vern Stephens, the man Veeck had wanted, to the Boston Red Sox instead. Veeck did some quick and tricky maneuvering. He returned to Cleveland, but he did not announce that the trade was off. Instead, he pretended to let the fans decide Boudreau's fate.

He rushed to the downtown area. There he toured the street corners and bars, telling the fans, "If you really want Lou, we'll keep him." By the time Veeck was finished, he had convinced the fans that *they* had been responsible for stopping the trade. Once more Veeck was a popular man in Cleveland.

What the fans didn't know, however, was that Veeck had written a clause into Boudreau's contract stating that if the Indians didn't have a good season in 1948, Lou could be demoted from playing-manager to player. But Boudreau need not have worried. Lou had a fabulous season in 1948. He batted .355, knocked in 106 runs and was voted the Most Valuable Player in the American League. Veeck was happy indeed that he hadn't made the trade.

When the season started, the Indians were not considered serious pennant contenders. But Cleveland got off to a fast start. A record-breaking opening-day crowd of 73,163 watched Feller throw a two-hitter against St. Louis. Lemon then beat Detroit, 8-2. Feller came back to beat the Tigers, 4-1. The Indians won six straight before they were stopped.

Cleveland then fell into a slump, losing four in a row. It soon became apparent that Feller was not going to have his usual great season. Actually, Feller did finish with a 19-15 record, but this was far below a typical "Rapid Robert" performance. Thus, with Feller in a slump, Boudreau needed pitching help. He turned to Gene Bearden. The rookie got his first start on May 8 against Washington. He won, 8-1, and went on to establish himself as Cleveland's most dependable starter.

On May 31, the Indians moved back into first place. The pennant race had boiled down to a four-team fight between Cleveland, Detroit, Boston and Philadelphia. Lemon, who was pitching marvelously, gave the team a big lift in late May by hurling a no-hitter against Detroit. But no team could gain a commanding lead in the race.

Because of the Indians' great performance, the fans were pouring into Cleveland's huge Municipal Stadium. The whole town was going wild over the team. Veeck continued to provide gifts, special nights, and stunt men as well as good baseball. The fans enjoyed every minute of it. On June 20, the Indians drew 82,781 spectators for a double-header against Philadelphia. This was larger than any previous crowd in baseball history. Veeck walked down to a box near the dugout, took the public address microphone and made the announcement. There was a huge roar. "The fans," Veeck explained later, "identified not only with our victories on the field but with our victories at the box office."

To show his gratitude, Veeck held "Joe Earley Night." Joe Earley was a night watchman at a local factory. He had written a letter asking why ballclubs had nights in honor of high-salaried players instead of in honor of ordinary fans like himself. So Veeck decided to make Joe Earley symbolic of all the loyal Indians' fans and hold a night in his honor.

Veeck presented Joe Earley with numerous gifts.

Many of the gifts were jokes. As the crowd cheered, Joe received an outhouse, an old fashioned trick car that reared up on its back wheels and exploded, a dozen chickens, and an old swayback horse. But Veeck also gave Joe some valuable gifts, including a refrigerator, a washing machine, a wrist watch, and luggage.

The rest of the fans were not forgotten on Joe Earley Night. Veeck even gave the 20,000 women in the crowd orchids. Veeck was so popular with the people of Cleveland that a few weeks later they gave *him* a night. It was probably the first, and only, time an owner was honored by the fans.

On July 9, to strengthen his pitching staff, Veeck made another daring move. He signed Leroy "Satchel" Paige, the legendary black pitcher. No one knew how old Paige really was. He seemed to have been pitching in the Negro Leagues and for countless troupes of barnstorming All-Stars for as long as anyone could remember. Until now the color barrier had kept him out of organized baseball. But during the off-season, Paige had pitched against many All-Star teams composed of big league stars and he had impressed them tremendously. In fact, Paige was considered one of the best pitchers in the business. Some people thought he might have been 65 years old. Actually he was well into his forties. But he had been pitching almost every day for thirty years in the United States, Canada, and Latin America.

Boudreau had told Veeck that he wasn't interested in Paige. Lou had heard that the old pitcher's arm was no longer strong enough. But Veeck brought Paige to Cleveland secretly. Long before game time one day he slipped Paige into a uniform and then asked Boudreau if he would mind taking a little batting practice against a youngster Veeck was considering signing. When Lou walked out on the field and saw Paige, he was so surprised he almost fell over.

But Boudreau was even more surprised when he had finished swinging at twenty pitches from Satchel Paige. Nineteen of the pitches were in the strike zone and Boudreau didn't get anything that resembled a base hit. Finally the embarrassed manager turned to Veeck and said, "Don't let him get away. We can use him."

This time Boudreau was correct. Paige, working both as a starter and a reliever, won six games and lost only one. His earned run average of 2.48 was the second best in the league. Paige was also a great drawing card. Wherever he pitched, people came out in droves. More than 60,000 watched him in Chicago. There was a "Standing Room Only" crowd in Detroit when it was mistakenly announced that Satch was going to pitch. In Cleveland, 78,382 turned out to see him throw a 1-0 three-hitter against the White Sox.

Paige was a humorous character. He told reporters that his best pitch was a *be ball*, because "it be where I want it to be." He also had names for his other pitches: the whipsy-dipsy-do, the single curve, the double curve, the triple curve, the hesitation pitch, the eephus, and the crossfire. Actually, Paige didn't have much of a breaking ball at all. His real forte was perfect control.

Although Satch was very popular with the other Indian players, he was a constant headache for Boudreau. Paige had no concept of time. He had always traveled at whatever pace he found comfortable, and he probably thought he was too old to change even though he was in the major leagues.

The old pitcher missed buses, trains, planes and sometimes entire games. He might show up in the afternoon for a night game—or in the evening for a day game. Finally Boudreau gave him a Cleveland schedule and said, "I'm going to ask you for this every day. If you are ever without it, it'll be an automatic $100 fine." Satch held onto the schedule, but his punctuality was not noticeably improved.

As the pennant race heated up, it became clear that Boudreau was the man who might carry Cleveland all the way. Each day he seemed to come up with another sensational feat. Once, when he had used so many players that he had run out of catchers, Lou put himself behind the plate for two innings. He handled the catching chores well enough for the Indians to hang onto a victory.

Another time Boudreau stole home against the Red Sox. Boston catcher Matt Batts was sure Lou was out and lost his temper when the umpire called Boudreau safe. The catcher became so involved in the argument with the umpire that he forgot Cleveland's Eddie Robinson was on first base. While Batts screamed, Robinson trotted unnoticed down to second base. Joe McCarthy, the Boston manager, was so furious at Batts that he ran out of the dugout and kicked the catcher in the seat of his pants.

On August 8 the pennant race was so close that only two percentage points separated the Indians, Yankees and Athletics. The Red Sox, in fourth place, were only one and a half games behind. That day the Indians and Yankees clashed in a double-header. Boudreau could not play. He had been out of the lineup for three days after injuring his leg and shoulder in a base-path collision. From the bench, he watched glumly as the Yankees jumped to a 6-2 lead in the opening game. Then, in the last of the seventh, Keltner walked and utility infielder Johnny Berardino hit a home run. The Yankee lead had been cut to two runs. Hegan continued the assault with a single. Clark walked and Mitchell singled to load the bases. The Yankees brought in their best relief pitcher, Joe Page.

In the dugout, Boudreau decided that he needed a right handed pinch hitter. But he had used all his available substitutes. Suddenly he pulled a bat from the bat rack and limped up the dugout steps. Over 70,000 fans began screaming when they realized that the injured manager was going to pinch hit. Lou did not disappoint the fans. He lined a single to left field, driving in the tying runs. Cleveland went on to sweep the doubleheader.

Still there were many who doubted that the Indians could win the pennant. Cleveland teams had a history of folding in the final drive. "Don't worry about the Indians, cracked Philadelphia coach Al Simmons, "they'll fall apart. They always do."

As the pennant race moved into September, the Indians dropped four and a half games behind. But Boudreau rallied the team again. Gordon went on a hitting binge, Bearden began winning almost every time he pitched, and Veeck used every trick he could think of to help the club. The grounds keeper at Municipal Stadium was instructed by Veeck to landscape the infield to favor the Indians. Because Boudreau had bad ankles and couldn't run quickly, the grass in front of shortstop was allowed to grow high and the ground was heavily watered to slow the ball down. Gordon was adept at starting the doubleplay, so the grass in front of his second-base position was kept short and the dirt was packed hard so the ball would get to him more quickly. Veeck also had the grounds keeper move the fences. Against power-hitting teams he secretly moved the fences back. But when the Indians played teams which had fewer long-ball hitters, the fences were moved in.

Slowly the Indians fought their way back into the race. On September 22 Feller beat the Red Sox, 5-2, and the Indians pushed into a tie for first place. For the next few days Cleveland kept winning. With just three games remaining in the season, the Indians led by two games over the second-place Red Sox. The Athletics and Yankees had finally been eliminated. If the Indians could keep winning, the pennant was theirs.

But Lemon lost the opener of a three-game series against Detroit, and the Red Sox won—cutting the Cleveland lead to a single game. The next day Bearden, ignoring tremendous pressure, pitched his second shutout of the week as Cleveland beat Detroit, 8-0. The Red Sox won again, but the Indians needed to win only their final game of the regular season to be champions of the American League.

But the Indians didn't win the game. Feller was pounded to the showers. The Tigers won, 7-1. Meanwhile, Boston beat the Yankees, 10-5. Cleveland would have to meet the Red Sox in a single game play-off for the pennant.

On the train to the play-off game in Boston, Boudreau refused to tell the press the name of his starting pitcher. But the Indians had secretly decided on Bearden at a grim clubhouse meeting after their defeat by Detroit. "This is your game," Boudreau had told his team. "I'd like to hear your suggestions about our pitcher for tomorrow."

Joe Gordon jumped up. "Lou," he said, "you've taken us this far. We're with you all the way. You name the pitcher."

The other players nodded in agreement. "All right," said Boudreau, "it will be Bearden. But don't tell anybody. Let's keep the Red Sox guessing."

The next day in Boston the tension was almost overpowering. The entire season depended on one game. To confuse the Red Sox, Boudreau had ordered Lemon and Feller to get rubdowns in the clubhouse as though they were going to pitch. Bearden, always calm, just sat on the dugout steps during batting practice. Then, a few minutes before game time, he startled everyone by beginning to warm up.

The game was a big one for every player. But it was especially vital to Boudreau. He had convinced himself that Veeck would remove him as manager if the Indians didn't win the pennant. So Boudreau, who had personally led his team all season, took matters into his own hands again. In the first inning he drilled a home run over the left-field wall. Boston came back to tie the score and the game remained 1-1 until the top of the fourth when Boudreau led off with a single. Gordon singled. With runners on first and second, Lou was tempted to order Ken Keltner to bunt. Instead he let the slugging third baseman hit away. Keltner justified Lou's faith by slamming a three-run homer.

As the game moved along, Cleveland pulled into a commanding lead while Bearden continued to stifle the Boston attack. Boudreau hit another home run. The manager finished the afternoon with two homers, two singles and an intentional walk. He was truly the Most Valuable Player in the league.

When Keltner fielded a ground ball and threw it

Jubilant Cleveland players carry pitcher Gene Bearden off the field after their playoff victory over the Red Sox.

to Robinson for the third out in the last of the ninth, the Indians were champions of the American League. The final score was 8-3.

There was a wild victory party for the players that night in Boston. And there were parties all over jubilant Cleveland.

To the delight of their loyal fans, the Indians dominated the World Series played against the Boston Braves. Feller lost the first game, 1-0 because an umpire was out of position and did not see that Bob had successfully picked a runner off second base. The next batter drove that runner home with the only run of the afternoon. But the Indians roared back the next day as Lemon won, 4-1. Bearden pitched the third game, in Cleveland, and shut out the Braves, 2-0.

Cleveland took the fourth game, 2-1. But Feller lost again in game five. The Braves clobbered him, 11-5. Still, the 86,288 Cleveland fans got a thrill when old Satchel Paige came in as a relief pitcher and retired the side in order in the seventh inning.

The Series then moved back to Boston. The Indians knew they would have to win on the road if they were to be champions. Lemon started the sixth game and pitched well. Gordon homered in the sixth inning to snap a 1-1 tie. Cleveland took the lead, 4-1, going into the last of the eighth. Then Lemon tired and the desperate Braves battled back. Boston scored twice and was threatening to take the lead when Boudreau waved to the bullpen. In walked Gene Bearden. The Braves' threat quickly ended. They couldn't handle Gene's knuckle ball. Bearden set Boston down again in the ninth. Cleve-

Timely infield moves by Boudreau (throwing) and Gordon (ducking) give the Indians a double play in the Series.

land won, 4-3. The Indians were champions at last.

In the clubhouse Boudreau kept repeating, "It was Bearden. He was the big man in the Series!"

The victory party on the train back to Cleveland that night was even more boisterous than the celebration after the Indians had won the pennant.

Veeck wound up with a bill from the railroad for $3,000 worth of damages. But he was too happy to care about anything but the victory—and the Cleveland fans felt the same way. The Indians had not won a pennant since 1920. The town had been waiting a long time to celebrate. Some 200,000 people lined the streets as the tired but delighted players rolled through the city in a horn-blowing motorcade. One year later, Veeck would have to solemnly bury the pennant flag in center field, for the Indians did not repeat as champions. In fact, the Indians have not won a World Series since then. But, in 1948, Cleveland made the most of its victory.

1955 Brooklyn Dodgers

"THIS IS NEXT YEAR"

There have never been fans like those who rooted for the old Brooklyn Dodgers before their move to Los Angeles. Loud, loyal, often eccentric, they withstood defeat and disappointment year after year. Some seasons the Dodgers finished deep down in the standings. Other years the team blew the pennant or got into the World Series only to lose at that stage of the game. But whatever the circumstances for their team's failure, the Brooklyn fans loyally waited for the day their beloved team would fly the World Championship flag over Ebbets Field. Setbacks only made their annual rallying cry more vocal: "Wait till next year!"

The Brooklyn Dodgers were the only team that did not represent an actual city (although teams like the Minnesota Twins now represent whole states). Brooklyn is merely one of New York City's five subdivisions, called boroughs. At the time the Dodgers played there, however, the 2.7 million population of Brooklyn Borough was larger than that of all but two major-league cities. And the Dodgers helped give the people of Brooklyn an identity and community spirit all their own.

The fans jammed into dilapidated little Ebbets Field, ringing cow bells, playing musical instruments and waving handkerchiefs at the umpires. One fan became so unbalanced by his devotion to the team that he shot to death a rival New York Giant rooter who had made an insulting wisecrack about the Dodgers.

During the 1920s and 1930s, Brooklyn had one of the worst teams in baseball. The Dodgers were so bad that their own fans nicknamed them "The Bums." Dodger outfielders got bopped on the head by fly balls. And one day three confused Dodger base runners all found themselves on third base at the same time. Needless to say, two were tagged out.

A few days later a cab driver, upon pulling up at Ebbets Field, shouted up to a fan in the grandstand, "What's the score?"

"We're losin', 2-1," yelled the fan. "But we got three men on base."

The cab driver asked, cynically, "Which base?"

By the 1940s, however, the Dodgers began to build a powerful dynasty and finally earn respect. In 1941 they won the pennant. They won again in 1947, and again in 1949, 1952 and 1953. In three other seasons they were not eliminated from the pennant race until the final day of the regular schedule. Each year, however, when the Dodgers reached the World Series, the result was the same. They lost. And each time they were defeated by the New York Yankees. As a result, the faithful Dodger fans began to repeat an annual threat, "Wait till next year."

The 1955 Dodgers put together one of the most powerful lineups in baseball history. Among the best hitters were (from left) Duke Snider, Gil Hodges, Jackie Robinson, Pee Wee Reese, and Roy Campanella.

The 1955 Dodgers entered the season with a team built around eight great veterans who had led the Dodgers to an eight-year winning surge. Jackie Robinson, the first black player in the major leagues, was at third base. Jackie had broken the color barrier in baseball when he joined the Dodgers in 1947, and in the process he had endured vulgar racial insults. Countless "beanballs" had been thrown at his head. But the former football star from UCLA was a man of iron will, burning determination and just plain guts. Despite the obstacles in his path, he had become a great star.

Robinson had hit over .300 for six consecutive seasons. Twice he had led the league in stolen bases, and he had won the Rookie of the Year and Most Valuable Player awards. His daring base running had captured the imaginations of fans throughout the league.

Proud, intelligent and outspoken, Robinson fought for his rights on the field once he established himself in the majors. He also feuded with the Brooklyn management off the field. He had become a hero to all black people and a spokesman for his race.

Pee Wee Reese, the Dodgers' captain, was the shortstop. Nicknamed "The Little Colonel," the five-foot ten-inch Kentuckian had joined the Dodgers in 1941 and immediately became one of baseball's finest shortstops. A clutch hitter and graceful fielder, Reese was the only Brooklyn star who hadn't been developed in the Dodger farm system. Brooklyn gave the Boston Red Sox $150,000 and five players for Pee Wee while he was still a minor leaguer. But Pee Wee proved to be a bargain. His popularity alone drew fans through the turnstiles.

Reese was popular even with his opponents. Once, after a Dodger player had hit a home run, a Cincinnati pitcher signaled to his catcher that he was going to knock down the next batter by throwing at his head. That batter happened to be Reese. Just as the pitcher released the ball, the catcher whispered, "Better get down on this one, Pee Wee." With this warning, Reese was able to duck in plenty of time.

Sparkplug Reese starts a double play against the Reds.

At first base was Gil Hodges, a muscular slugger whose huge hands and quick reflexes allowed him to field his position superbly. Hodges had hit 200 home runs in the six seasons leading up to 1955 and averaged over 100 RBIs per year. Hodges was a quiet, modest man. He had married a Brooklyn girl and was one of the few Dodgers who lived in Brooklyn the year round. He became the fans' favorite player. During the 1952 World Series, when Gil was in a slump, Brooklyn ministers and rabbis led special prayers for him.

The catcher, Roy Campanella, was a black man

who followed Robinson into the majors and later followed him into the Hall of Fame. "Campy" was a squat but powerful player with real punch at the plate. For years he had been the best catcher in the National League. He won the league's Most Valuable Player award in 1951 and 1953. Many of his teammates called Campanella the "Good Humor Man" because of the funny, folksy stories he told about his days in the fly-by-night Negro leagues, where he had played before being allowed in the majors.

Carl Furillo, the right-fielder, was a tough Italian whose powerful throwing arm earned him the nickname "The Rifle." Furillo was the team's most underrated star, but he had a lifetime batting average of .299 and won the batting title in 1953.

By Furillo's side in the outfield was the great center fielder, Duke Snider. "The Duke of Flatbush" was the Dodgers' only prominent left-handed hitter. For years he had been belting the ball over the towering right-field scoreboard into Brooklyn's Bedford Avenue. There, young boys with baseball gloves stood in the street with portable radios pressed against their ears, waiting for Snider to send them a souvenir.

Snider was a complex man. Sometimes he was the team comedian. During batting practice he would put on two caps, with the peaks pointed in opposite directions. At other times he was sullen and withdrawn, especially when he was in a slump or criticized by the sportswriters, who believed that Snider should have been even greater than he was. Nevertheless, Snider was a superstar. He could climb the center-field wall to thwart home runs, and his quick, whiplike swing had produced 186 home runs and four .300-plus seasons after he became a regular in 1949.

The aces of the Brooklyn pitching staff were veterans Don Newcombe and Carl Erskine. "Newk" stood six feet four inches and weighed more than 225 pounds. He was an overpowering pitcher with a blazing fast ball. Although sometimes moody and emotional, Newcombe was the Dodgers' big winner. Erskine was a very religious man and a leader, the team's player representative. Although he didn't have great speed on his pitches, he was a careful student of the art of pitching.

"When he is right," said Fresco Thompson, the Dodgers' Vice-President, "watching Erskine is like watching an artist painting a picture. He has a reason for every pitch." Carl had set a World Series strikeout record in 1953 and had won sixty-eight games in his four previous major league seasons.

But for all their individual heroics and skills, the Dodgers had never been able to collect baseball's biggest prize—the World Series championship. When the Dodgers started spring training at Vero Beach, Florida, in 1955 it didn't appear that their luck would change. Manager Walter Alston was under heavy pressure. He had been hired the previous season to bring a World Series victory to Brooklyn. Instead, the Dodgers hadn't even reached the Series. They finished a distant second behind the rival New York Giants. Many fans and sportswriters thought that Alston, a withdrawn, colorless man, should not be rehired. But Walter O'Malley,

Manager Walter Alston was under pressure to win big in 1955.

the Dodgers' owner, signed Alston to another one-year contract. This time Alston had to win.

Alston's team, however, seemed to be in a shambles. Robinson, who was having trouble with his legs, was thirty-six years old. Pee Wee Reese was also thirty-six. Both aging stars were slowing down. Campanella, thirty-three, had suffered a nerve injury in his hand in 1954. He had been forced to swing the bat virtually one-handed and his average had slipped to .207. No one knew if he could regain his old form again.

Erskine had been bothered by arm trouble. Newcombe, who had won seventeen games in 1949, nineteen in 1950, and twenty in 1951, had returned to Brooklyn in 1954 after two years in the Army. He couldn't seem to get anybody out. In 1954 Newk had won only nine games.

Another problem was Billy Loes, a young right-hander who had never quite fulfilled his great potential. Although Loes had won forty games in three years, he was forever talking about how much he disliked baseball. He had a theory that it was not good to win *too many* games in a season because the club would expect him to win a lot of games the next year, too. Loes was a champion at making up excuses for poor plays. Once he told reporters that he had fumbled a ball because the sun was in his eyes—a highly improbable occurrence since it had been hit along the ground.

Johnny Podres, another young pitcher, had been operated on for appendicitis during the winter and his immediate future seemed questionable.

Among the non-pitchers, only Hodges, Furillo and Snider were assured of starting positions.

Without a set starting lineup, the Dodgers were a confused, bickering group in Florida. Robinson, who disliked Alston, was angered when the manager began using a cocky rookie named Don Hoak at third base. "How can I get in condition to play ball if Alston won't let me in the lineup?" Robinson snapped. "I can't talk to him man-to-man."

Hard-hitting Campanella was insulted when the manager placed him eighth in the batting order. Pitcher Russ Meyer, who had won thirteen games in 1954, complained that he wasn't pitching enough. Second baseman Jim "Junior" Gilliam, noting that rookie Don Zimmer was often stationed at second base, worried that he was about to be traded. Zimmer was a tough little guy who had overcome a serious head injury (he had been hit by a pitch in the minor leagues) and was determined to make the Dodgers' squad. He dreamed of succeeding Reese at shortstop. "If I ever get in the lineup," he said confidently, "they'll never get me out."

Actually, the Dodgers *had* tried to trade Gilliam to the Cincinnati Reds for left-fielder Wally Post, but the deal fell through. Left field remained Alston's biggest problem. The manager considered switching Robinson, Gilliam or even the agile Hodges to the outfield. His first choice was a little Cuban named Sandy Amoros. But Amoros was in trouble with the Brooklyn management. He had arrived at training camp three days late. "I got lost," Amoros explained to Dodger Vice President Buzzi Bavasi.

"He must think I'm a fool," Bavasi rasped. "He got off the boat in Miami and started to drive up here to Vero Beach. How could he have gotten lost? If he turned right he'd fall into the Atlantic Ocean. If he turned left he'd fall into the Everglades."

Bavasi fined Amoros $100. When Sandy heard the news he smiled. Amoros' English wasn't very good and he thought Bavasi was *giving* him $100.

But from all this confusion emerged one of the strongest teams in National League history. Alston finally settled on an infield of Hodges, Gilliam, Reese and Robinson. Furillo, Snider and Amoros— finally back in management's good graces—were in the outfield. Campanella, his hand completely healed, was behind the plate. The pitching staff was deep with starters. Veteran Clem Labine, fastballer Karl Spooner, and dependable Ed Roebuck gave Brooklyn an excellent bullpen.

A tough conditioning program, which Alston had employed in Florida, began to pay off right away. The Dodgers thumped Pittburgh, 6-1, on opening day and then romped past the Giants, the Philadelphia Phillies, and Pittsburgh Pirates to pile up seven more victories in a row. They returned to Ebbets Field and tied a modern major league record of nine consecutive victories at the start of the season by beating Philadelphia. The following day they pounded the Phillies, 14-4, to break the record. Robinson, Snider, Amoros and Zimmer hit home runs. Zimmer and Furillo had four hits each. Brooklyn had won ten straight. But the players were puzzled. Only 3,874 fans had attended the Dodger-Phillie game.

During the game, owner O'Malley had decided to reward the few fans who had come to watch the team break the record. The public-address announcer told the crowd that he would have a special announcement after the game. The message was that a commemorative ashtray would be sent to everyone who turned in a ticket stub from the game. But, in the clubhouse, Snider made a prophetic remark when he snapped, "I thought they were going to announce that the franchise had been moved to Los Angeles."

The players and management were wrong, however, to think that Brooklyn fans had abandoned them. Most fans were watching the games on television. All the Dodger home games were being televised. Actually, attendance over the season was not so bad anyway. Brooklyn still drew over one million fans to its tiny park—the second best attendance figure in the league.

Over 27,000 showed up the next evening. But the Giants broke the Dodgers' winning streak. Brooklyn didn't go down without a fight, however. Alston and Zimmer were thrown out of the game for arguing with the umpires. Jackie Robinson ignited some fireworks, too. After Giant pitcher Sal Maglie, the Dodgers' most hated enemy, threw a fastball close to his head, Jackie responded on the next pitch by bunting down the first base line. Hoping that Maglie would come over to field the ball, Robinson planned to run the Giant star down if Maglie got close to the baseline. But the Giants' first baseman took the bunt instead. He tossed to second baseman Davey Williams, who was covering first base. Robinson, ready to mow down anyone in a Giant uniform, plowed into Williams, knocking him toward right field. Players from both dugouts rushed onto the field. They waved fists and exchanged words but the umpires finally calmed things down.

There was more trouble in the fifth inning. Giant shortstop Alvin Dark hit a right-field drive that should have been a double. But Dark didn't want a double. He wanted Robinson. Dark wheeled around second and charged toward Jackie at third. Furillo's rifle arm beat Dark by fifteen feet, but Dark crashed into Robinson with a football block, jarring the ball from Jackie's hands. Both players rose from the ground snarling. Only quick action by the umpires prevented a riot.

Baseball crowds came alive when Jackie Robinson was on base. Here, he slides home safely against the Chicago Cubs.

Brooklyn lost two out of three to the Giants. But it was only a temporary slowdown in the pennant quest. The Dodgers rolled past the Cincinnati Reds, Chicago Cubs, Milwaukee Braves and St. Louis Cardinals. By May 5 the Dodgers' record was seventeen wins and two losses. They were in first place by seven and a half games. The pennant race was practically over before it had really begun.

On May 5, Walter Alston proved, once and for all, that he was the unchallenged boss of the Brooklyn Dodgers. Newcombe had refused to pitch batting practice that day. Alston was on the field when pitching coach Joe Becker emerged from the clubhouse to tell him of Newcombe's announcement. "He says he doesn't want to," Becker told the surprised manager. "He says he only wants to pitch in games."

Alston stormed into the clubhouse, where he found the big pitcher sitting in front of his locker. "I hear you don't want to pitch batting practice," he said, his voice cold and hard.

"That's right," said Newcombe.

"Take off that uniform and get out of the park," Alston exploded. "You're suspended!"

The next day Newcombe returned to apologize. He was fined $300 plus a day's pay. And he still had to pitch batting practice. After that, the Dodgers never questioned Alston's authority. In fact, Newcombe suddenly began pitching as he had before he went into the Army. He was unbeatable. Against the Cubs, Newcombe pitched a one-hitter. He faced just twenty-seven batters (the minimum for a nine inning game). Gene Baker, the only man to reach base, was thrown out stealing after he singled. The Dodgers were really rolling.

The Dodgers won twenty-two of their first twenty-four games. By mid-June they were ten and a half games ahead of the second-place team. Newcombe's record was ten wins and no losses. Alston was using Newk as a pinch hitter, too, for he was an excellent hitting pitcher. Newcombe responded by batting over .400 much of the season.

Campanella had knocked in more than fifty runs by the first week in June. Campy, Hodges and Snider were battling for the home run leadership in the league. Robinson, Reese and Gilliam were coming up with clutch hits. Erskine, Loes and Meyer were also winning. On June 11, as the Dodgers ripped apart the Milwaukee Braves, Snider hit three home runs and a double.

Then the Dodgers ran into unexpected trouble. Robinson and Campanella suffered knee injuries. When Jackie tried to come back too soon, his knee buckled during batting practice. Snider, who had hit thirty-five home runs through July, caught a virus. He was so weak he hit just seven more homers during the rest of the season. Amoros, who had been hitting close to .300, hurt his back. The pitching staff suddenly resembled a hospital ward. Meyer suffered a fractured collarbone. Erskine, Podres, Loes and Spooner all had sore arms.

But nothing could stop the Dodgers from winning. Alston moved Gilliam to left field, Zimmer went to second base and Hoak went to third. All the youngsters hit well. Zimmer finished the season with fifteen home runs.

In the first two months of the 1955 season, Roy Campanella knocked in more than fifty runs.

To bolster the pitching staff, Alston dipped into the minor leagues. He called up two young pitchers —Roger Craig from the Montreal Royals and Don Bessent from the St. Paul Saints. When the two rookies arrived on a Sunday morning, they were greeted by a surprise: they were both scheduled to start in a doubleheader against Cincinnati that day.

To the amazement of everyone—including themselves—the rookie pitchers won their ballgames.

Later, Alston even turned to a nineteen-year-old rookie who had sat on the bench all season and done little more than pitch batting practice. The rookie had received a large bonus and, under the rule at that time, bonus players had to be kept on the big league roster for two years. So he sat on the bench. He hadn't started a game in fifty days. The rookie's name was Sandy Koufax.

One day Koufax would become the greatest left-hander in Dodger history, but then he was a frightened youngster. When coach Jake Pitler learned that Koufax was going to start against the slugging Cincinnati Reds, he groaned, "Oh no!"

But everything was going right for Alston and the Dodgers that season—even Koufax. Sandy shut out the Reds, 7-0, and struck out fourteen men. He pitched another shutout in his next start. Koufax was still too inexperienced to pitch much more after that. Yet he had come through when his teammates needed him.

The Dodgers became a friendly, close-knit team. The veterans had been together for years. Even rookies like Koufax were made to feel welcome. "It's a good clubhouse," said Campanella. "It's a bunch of guys appreciating and respecting each other."

"Everybody helps everybody else," Hodges explained. "We've watched each other so long that when one of us goes into a slump the others have a pretty good idea what he is doing wrong. It's been a pleasure being with all of them so long."

There were some squabbles, of course. Snider lashed out at the booing fans one night, charging that "Brooklyn fans are the worst in baseball. They don't deserve a pennant." He apologized the next day. Campanella and Robinson were never very friendly. Robinson thought Campy should have been more outspoken on racial matters. Newcombe lost his temper occasionally. The night Brooklyn clinched the pennant, Newk became furious when Snider celebrated by pouring a can of beer in Newcombe's new Panama hat.

But for the most part it was a congenial, confident group. Reese was the elder statesman and social chairman. He arbitrated many problems. The other players had stools in front of their lockers. But Pee Wee sat in an old black armchair. "Somebody has to be disgruntled if only nine men can play," he would say. "But there is no jealousy here. We always have had harmony. Always."

Much of the fun in the clubhouse was supplied by Charlie DiGiovanna, the batboy. Actually, Charlie was not a boy. He was twenty-five years old and probably the oldest batboy in baseball. The players called him "The Brow" because of his bushy eyebrows. They liked him so much they always voted him a half share of their World Series money. One day Charlie became so involved in a ballgame that he started screaming at the umpire from his place in the dugout. He quickly found himself kicked out of a game!

Charlie would walk through the clubhouse goading the players to sign their quota of autographed baseballs. "Everybody *loves* to sign," he would sing out. But there always seemed to be a lot of unsigned baseballs. So Charlie became an expert forger. In fact, he could copy perfectly the signature of every player on the team.

The other clubhouse character was equipment

man John Griffin. The Dodgers called him "The Senator," because he resembled the stereotype of a politician—fat belly, pudgy face and a cigar sticking out of his mouth. Griffin, who had been with the team over forty years, kept the players laughing by wearing outlandish outfits. He wore ladies' hats, stovepipe hats, coonskin caps, derbies and football helmets in the clubhouse—and sometimes in the middle of crowded hotel lobbies. He would wear the same outfit as long as the team kept winning. He felt it brought good luck. One day he showed up with a baby's hat, diaper, bib and rattle. Another time he was spotted outside a fancy hotel wearing a beanie with a propeller on top and the ever-present cigar stuffed in his mouth.

As the season moved into September, the Dodgers pulled farther and farther away from the opposition. On September 5, a crowd of 33,451 turned out to wish the Dodgers luck as they closed a home stand and headed for their final, long road trip. That day, as the fans screamed with delight, Newcombe won his twentieth game and set a league record for pitchers by smacking his seventh homer of the year. Snider belted his forty-second homer to tie a club record.

Three days later in Milwaukee, the Dodgers clobbered the Braves, 10-2, and clinched the pennant. No National League team had ever before clinched a pennant so early in the season. It was their twelfth victory in thirteen games. Snider climbed atop a table and delivered a toast to "the greatest bunch of guys I've ever known." Then the Dodgers celebrated until dawn.

Campanella greets Snider after a home run. The Dodgers held lots of celebrations like that at home plate in 1955.

Brooklyn entered the World Series with an awesome list of accomplishments. The Dodgers had finished thirteen and a half games in front of the second-place Braves. The hitters had led the league in batting average, home runs, runs, and pinch-hitting. Their 201 home runs combined for the third best total in history. The pitching corps had the lowest earned-run average in the league, as well as the most strikeouts.

Campanella, whose career had seemed in jeopardy during spring training, was named the Most Valuable Player in the league for the third time. He hit .318 with thirty-two home runs and 107 runs batted in. Furillo hit .314 with twenty-six homers.

Hodges knocked in 102 runs. Snider was the league RBI leader with 136. Robinson, who missed a third of the season because of his ailing legs, still stole twelve bases in fifteen attempts.

Newcombe's pinch hitting average was .381. His mound record was just as impressive as his hitting. He won twenty games and lost only five. Erskine was 11-8, Bessent 8-1, Craig 5-3 and Loes 10-4. Clem Labine, the best relief pitcher in the majors, appeared in sixty games, including fifty-two in relief. Unscored upon in thirty-five appearances, his record was 13-5.

But Brooklyn still had to beat the New York Yankees in the World Series. The Yanks, as usual, were favored. The Dodgers' former third baseman, Billy Cox, left no doubt about why the Yankees were expected to win. "The Dodgers will choke up," he said. "I know, I was with them. They always choked up as soon as they heard they had to play the Yankees."

When the Series opened at Yankee Stadium, it appeared that Cox was right. Brooklyn took an early lead only to see Newcombe fall apart. The Dodgers trailed, 6-3, after seven innings. But the Dodgers fought back. They scored a run in the top of the eighth and moved Robinson over to third base with one out. From there, as 63,869 fans looked on in disbelief, the aging Robinson tried a daring steal of home plate. He looked like the Jackie Robinson of his younger days, scoring in a cloud of dust. Suddenly Brooklyn trailed by just one run.

During the ninth inning, Snider singled to put the tying run on base. The crowd was roaring. Relief pitcher Bob Grim of the Yankees faced Campanella with one out. Campy swung and the ball headed toward the stands. But Joe Collins, New York's right-fielder, pushed back against the wall to catch Campanella's drive. Furillo then struck out. New York had won the first game, 6-5.

Afterward, everyone was talking about Robinson's steal. "It was a lousy play," said Yankee catcher Yogi Berra. "The Dodgers were two runs behind when he did it. That run didn't mean nothin'."

But Berra had overlooked the psychological effect the steal of home had on the Yankee pitchers. Now, every time Robinson was on base, they had to worry that he might steal. The Dodgers were also affected by Robinson's sensational feat. It helped keep them from becoming demoralized, even after New York won the second game, 4-2. No team had ever lost the first two Series games and come back to win the championship, but the Dodgers still felt they had a chance.

The Series shifted to Brooklyn. Alston started young Johnny Podres, who was celebrating his twenty-third birthday that day. Podres, native of a little town called Weatherbee, New York, had posted a weak 9-10 record in the regular season. He had finished just five of his twenty-four starts. But he had a back problem and was getting stronger toward the end of the season.

Podres was more than ready. He allowed the Yankees only seven hits and beat them, 8-3. Campanella hit a two-run homer. But the star, once more, was Robinson. With the score tied, 2-2, in the bottom of the second, Jackie singled. Moments later the Dodgers had loaded the bases. Robinson, on third base, became a whirling dervish. He danced back and forth. He faked dash after dash toward home plate.

Bob Turley, the Yankee pitcher, became increasingly concerned that Robinson would once more steal home. He was unable to concentrate on Gilliam at the plate. He walked Gilliam on four straight pitches, forcing in Robinson with the lead run. Jackie's steal of home two days earlier had paid off.

In the seventh inning, Robinson continued his fearless base running as he humiliated the Yankees' young left fielder Elston Howard. Jackie doubled to left, took a wide turn around second and feinted as though he was going to dash toward third. Then he faked back toward second. Howard, who had the ball in left field, became so disconcerted he threw the ball behind Robinson—to second base. As soon as Howard released his throw, Jackie raced safely to third.

Amoros then dribbled a hit through the drawn-in infield. Robinson sped home to score. In the stands, Ty Cobb, the king of the old-time base runners, said with a chuckle, "Pardon me for saying this, but that's the way I used to run the bases."

Now the Dodgers were moving again. Snider, Campanella and Hodges hit home runs in the fourth game. Erskine was knocked out of the box, but Labine strode out of the bullpen to stop the Yankees and pick up an 8-5 victory. The Series was even.

The following day, Alston gambled again. This time his gamble was to start a rookie, Roger Craig.

Once more the manager's hunch paid off. Craig held the Yanks to two runs and four hits until he tired in the seventh. Labine again came in and protected the lead. Earlier, Snider had tied a Series record by hitting his third and fourth home runs and Amoros had also hit a homer. Craig was credited with a 5-3 victory. Brooklyn was just one game away from its first World Championship.

But the Dodgers still had to win at Yankee Stadium, where the rest of the Series would be played. Alston, whose pitching staff was decimated by exhaustion and tired arms, started young Karl Spooner —a solid reliefer during the season. Spooner had no luck as a starter. He was bombed out in the first inning as the Yankees banged out five runs. From then on Brooklyn's bullpen did an excellent job, but it was too late. The Dodger offense never got moving, and the Yanks won, 5-1. The teams would meet in a seventh and final game.

Podres started for the Dodgers. Tommy Byrne, a sixteen-game winner who had already beaten Brooklyn in the second game of the Series, pitched for the Yanks. The Dodgers were playing in the enemy's ballpark, but many of the 62,465 fans at Yankee Stadium were Dodger fans. And it seemed that every radio and television set in Brooklyn was tuned to the game. Would the fans once more have to say, "Wait till next year"?

The odds seemed to be weighted heavily against the Dodgers. Podres was pitching with only three days' rest. The Yanks' Byrne had had four days' rest. The proud Yankees had won all three of the Series games played at Yankee Stadium that year. And they had also won sixteen World Championships. The Dodgers had won none.

For three innings the pitchers were locked in a scoreless tie. The tension mounted. Then, in the fourth, Campanella slashed a double. He moved to third when Furillo grounded out. Byrne worked carefully against Hodges, but the slugger lined a hard single to left. Campy scored and the Dodgers led, 1-0.

In the sixth, Hodges drove in the Dodgers' second run with a sacrifice fly. But in the bottom of the sixth, Podres ran into trouble. The Yankees' Billy Martin led off with a walk. Gil McDougald beat out a bunt. New York had runners on first and second with no one out. Berra hit a high fly deep into the left-field corner. Dodger fans moaned. It appeared to be a sure double. Both runs would score if the ball dropped safely.

Luckily, Sandy Amoros was in left field for the Dodgers. In the top of the sixth, Alston had sent up a pinch-hitter for Zimmer. When the side was out, Gilliam, who had been playing left field, thus moved to second base for Zimmer and Amoros replaced Gilliam in the outfield.

Gilliam could never have caught the ball for he was a natural infielder playing out of position in left field. But somehow little Sandy Amoros—who had been positioned far off in deep left center against left-handed, pull-hitter Berra—dashed all the way into the left-field corner, where the foul line met the stands. He extended his bare hand to fend off the railing, then snared the ball in the webbing of his outstretched glove. It was an impossible catch—

The biggest surprise of the season was Johnny Podres, who made the difference between winning and losing in the Series.

one of the greatest in World Series history.

The Yankees had been so certain Amoros couldn't catch the fly that Martin and McDougald had been running almost since the crack of the bat. McDougald had already rounded second when Sandy made the catch. Amoros whirled and threw the ball to Reese. Pee Wee relayed to Hodges on first, who stretched off the bag for the ball while McDougald was still frantically trying to get back to the base. It was a double play. When Reese threw out the next batter, Hank Bauer, the inning was over.

But the Yankees continued to threaten. In the last of the eighth, with Podres obviously tiring, Phil Rizzuto singled. Then, with one out, McDougald hit a hard grounder to Don Hoak at third base. It seemed as if Hoak would be able to turn it into a double play. But the ball hit a pebble and bounced off Hoak's shoulder for a single. Rizzuto raced to third. Were the Dodgers about to lose again?

Podres made sure they didn't. He forced Berra to loft a fly to right field. Furillo charged in to make the catch. Rizzuto bluffed as though he was going to try to tag up from third and dash for the plate. But he was only bluffing. He didn't dare test "The Rifle's" arm. Bauer struck out, ending the inning. The Dodgers were just three outs away.

In the last of the ninth the Stadium seemed to tremble with excitement. Every Dodger player was on the top step of the dugout. The Yankees' Bill Skowron grounded out. Bob Cerv flied out. The Dodgers needed just one more out. Podres worked carefully against the dangerous Elston Howard. Elston swung and hit a ground ball to Reese. Pee Wee had been waiting for this moment since 1941. He fielded the ball and threw to Hodges. The Dodgers had finally won!

As the ball disappeared in Gil's huge glove, fans began to pour out onto the field. There was dancing and singing and tears of joy throughout the night in the streets of Brooklyn. "Next Year" had arrived.

1969 New York Mets

WE'RE NUMBER ONE

It stood to reason that the New York Mets would win their first World Series the same year that man took his initial step on the moon. For the Mets' own fans had often said that their chances of getting into a Series were as likely as man getting to the moon.

In July 1969, Apollo XI astronauts did indeed reach the moon and achieved a feat grateful Americans didn't expect to see until well into the 1970s, if then. Four months later, the Mets did indeed reach the World Series and achieved a feat grateful New Yorkers didn't expect to see until . . . well, maybe never.

Unlike the space program, the Mets' program had been synonymous with failure until 1969. The team came into existence, along with a Houston franchise, in 1962 when the National League expanded to ten teams. There had been a lack of National League baseball in New York City ever since the old Brooklyn Dodgers and their rivals, the New York Giants, abandoned the city for the West Coast in 1958. But while franchises were granted to two new teams in 1962, the existing teams made sure few good players were available. Houston and New York were allowed to draft major leaguers from the rosters of the other teams—but only after the best players had been safely protected.

The Mets' management didn't help its own cause much. Team officials sought well-known players so that they could compete at the box office with the American League Yankees, who were then baseball's great dynasty. Instead of seeking younger players with whom they could build for the future, the Mets reached into the grab bag and came up with aging veterans like Gil Hodges, an ex-Brooklyn Dodger hero who was near the end of his career. The team's first spring roster was filled with over-the-hill veterans and fringe players who hardly belonged in the major leagues.

The manager of this awful collection of culls and rejects was 71-year-old Casey Stengel, who had led the Yankees to ten pennants and seven World Series victories from 1949 to 1960. Stengel quickly realized that he would have to hide the Mets' flaws behind a smokescreen of funny sayings. Though he sometimes became so angry that he called them "frauds," more often Casey would say with a laugh, "Come see my amazin' Mets, which in some cases have played only semi-pro ball."

On the eve of the Mets' first game, played in St. Louis, there was an omen of things to come. Sixteen players got trapped in a hotel elevator for half an hour. The next day they lost to the Cardinals, 11-4. They went on to lose eight more games in a row. Their first-year record was an unimposing 40-120. "The Mets," observed Bill Veeck, who had once owned a pretty bad St. Louis Browns team himself, "are the worst team in baseball history."

The Mets became a national symbol of incompetence. Game after game was marked by kooky incidents. The team constantly lost because of horrendous errors and mental mistakes. Outfielders stood by as fly balls dropped between them. Infielders threw to the wrong bases. Batters watched as third strikes split the plate. Pitchers balked men home. And base runners specialized in forgetting to touch bases as they ran past.

No one typified the Mets' non-heroes better than first baseman Marv Throneberry. A monument to imperfection, he could always be counted upon to make a costly, but humorous, mistake. Once, during a game against Chicago, he failed to step aside after throwing the ball in a rundown play. The base runner was called safe as Marv was charged with interference. The Cubs took advantage of this misplay and went on to score four runs that inning. In the same inning, Throneberry tried to make up for his mistake by cracking an apparent two-run triple with two out. But as Marv stood on third, the Cubs' first baseman called for the ball and stepped on first. The umpire signaled Marv out for failing to touch the base, thus ending the inning and nullifying the runs. Stengel stormed from the dugout to protest. But first base coach Cookie Lavagetto intercepted him before he reached the umpire. "Quiet down, Case," said Cookie. "He didn't touch second base, either."

The fans nicknamed the bumbling Throneberry, "Marvelous Marv." They founded a "Marv Loser's Club" and wore T-shirts with the letters VRAM (Marv spelled backwards) across the chest.

In addition, the fans waved banners with clever

slogans like "Ninth Place or Bust" and "What Me Worry? I'm a Mets Fan." They would chant in unison "Let's Go Mets" in the final inning, even if the team was losing by ten runs—which it often was. While the Mets kept on dropping game after game, the fans kept pouring into the ballpark to root for the lovable losers. In fact, the Mets drew over two million fans in their first two seasons.

Some only laughed at their defeats. Others saw a philosophical connection. James Wechsler, a political columnist for the New York *Post*, interpreted the Mets as a source of identification for all people who considered themselves losers. "The Mets are a symbol," he wrote. "They embody the furtive hopes and desperate dreams of every underdog and lost soul in the universe . . . of every philosopher who sees man capable of rising above his limitations. . . ."

Indeed, the Mets had limitations. An example was Manager Stengel's search for a catcher for his bedraggled team. He tried one player who could hit but not throw. Then he found one who could throw but not hit. Finally he used a man who could hit and could throw. Unfortunately, the latter player could not catch.

After four straight years in tenth place, Stengel retired in 1965. He was replaced by Wes Westrum, who guided the team to ninth place in 1966. While they fell back to tenth in 1967, the arrival of a fine young pitcher named Tom Seaver gave the team its first glimmer of hope. Seaver won sixteen games and was named Rookie of the Year. In 1968 popular Gil Hodges, who had been managing the Washington Senators, replaced Westrum. The quiet but firm Hodges earned the respect of his players. He immediately began to mold a new look. Older play ers were discarded, providing opportunities for the younger men who were pouring out of the Mets' suddenly productive farm system.

The Mets finished ninth in 1968, but it was a strong ninth. The players' confidence was growing as Hodges got them to believe in themselves. The "new Mets" were not tied to the past. They were their own men. Remarkably in tune with the world, they dressed in mod fashions—Edwardian suits and bell-bottomed slacks—and thought for them-selves. Twenty-two of the players at spring training camp had attended college. They had a common purpose and were freed from cliques that had torn other Met clubs apart. For 1969, Hodges felt he had a respectable ballclub—to a degree.

The heart of the team was its pitching staff, po-tentially the best in baseball. No roster listed so many fine young pitchers. The best of the pitchers and the team leader was 24-year-old Seaver. The handsome Californian was mature, articulate, and especially competitive. "You can't overestimate what it means to have him as an influence on the club," Hodges said on several occasions. Just looking at Seaver's record at the end of the season, it was easy to see his tangible influence—he won twenty-five games and lost only seven.

Seaver was a right-hander. A left-hander who was almost as good was 25-year-old Jerry Koosman. He had come to the Mets, ironically, after being recom-mended to the club by a Shea Stadium usher, whose

The Mets began their climb to the top with young, strong-armed pitchers like Jerry Koosman.

son had played with Jerry on an army team at Fort
Bliss, Texas. Koosman showed exceptional promise as a rookie in 1968 by winning nineteen games. A
friendly, gangling farm boy from Minnesota, he
had learned to throw the ball in the family barn.
While he made such folksy comments as "I haven't
had so much fun since my third-grade picnic," he
was dead serious on the mound. In 1969, he posted
a 17-9 record and was the Mets' toughest pitcher
in the stretch run.

At one point in the season, Koosman and Seaver
combined to win nineteen of twenty decisions.

But the mound corps ran much deeper than these
two stars. Hodges had his choice of four other starters—Gary Gentry, Jim McAndrew, Don Cardwell,
and Nolan Ryan. Gentry, a rookie, usually got the
call in the starting rotation and finished with a 13-12
record. But the others were all capable of stepping
in and throwing hard. Ryan, a youngster with a
blazing fastball, was often used in relief, along with
veterans Tug McGraw, Ron Taylor, and Cal
Koonce. Ryan gained notoriety for a homespun
remedy for blisters on his pitching hand: he soaked
his fingers in a pickle brine. The old Mets would
have loved to see that!

Except for hitters Cleon Jones and Tommie Agee,
the rest of the Mets were not known for their fear-
some talents. But Hodges deftly juggled the lineup,
deploying left-handed hitters against right-handed
pitchers, and right-handed hitters against left-
handed pitchers. The manager thus kept the team
respectable at bat and strong in the field.

Hodges upset the canons of baseball by using

center fielder Agee, his best home run hitter in 1969 (with twenty-six), as the leadoff batter. Agee had been the American League Rookie of the Year for the Chicago White Sox in 1966, but then he lost his batting eye. The Sox traded him to the Mets before the start of the 1968 season. In their first six years, the Mets had tried twenty-seven different men in center field without success. In Agee, they felt they had the hitter and fielder who would end their search. But Tommie had a 0-for-34 slump early in the 1968 season and finished with a meager .217 average. His confidence seemed gone. In 1969, however, he found himself. Agee hit .271, ran the bases brilliantly, and became a first-rate leadoff man.

Jones, who had grown up with Agee in Mobile, Alabama, and gone to high school with him, had been a Met since 1963. He had hit .297 in 1968 but never quite fulfilled his promise of becoming a star.

Tommie Agee breaks up a double play against the Cubs. He developed a new spirit with the Mets.

Hodges, however, refused to give up on Jones. He encouraged him and talked openly of his potential. In 1969, Cleon hit .340 and almost led the National League in batting. Between them, Agee and Jones knocked in 151 runs.

Two others players, shortstop "Bud" Harrelson and catcher Jerry Grote, escaped Hodges' platoon system. A 145-pounder, Harrelson was in the mold of the old Mets when he tried out for the majors. For example, sportswriters had a pool going to guess the first time Bud would hit a ball out of the infield in his first spring training. He fooled them and went on to bat .248 for the season. His steady defense was never in question. Grote hit .252, respectable for a catcher, and won the confidence of the pitching staff.

Elsewhere in the infield, a fine youngster named Ken Boswell shared second base with no-hit, good-field Al Weis; aging Ed Charles shared third with young Wayne Garrett; and Don Clendenon, a thirty-four-year-old veteran acquired from the Montreal Expos, split the first-base duties with Ed Kranepool, one of the earliest Mets.

Hodges used three right-fielders—Ron Swoboda, Art Shamsky, and Rod Gaspar.

At spring training, Hodges predicted that the Mets would be contenders for the first time. The league had been divided into two six-team divisions. Gil expected the Met pitching to be good enough to carry the team as high as third place in the East, behind the defending champions, the St. Louis Cardinals, and the powerful Chicago Cubs. But the odds against the Mets' winning the pennant

Cleon Jones was a better player than ever after his old high school buddy, Tommie Agee, joined the Mets.

were 100-to-1. Even the players were realistic enough not to expect too much.

"Hey," Agee said to Jones at spring training, "wouldn't it be something if we won it all? That would shake 'em up."

Cleon just laughed. "It would shake me up, too!"

The season opened like every other Met season —with a defeat. The New Yorkers were beaten, 11-10, by the Montreal Expos, an expansion team making its major-league debut. For a while, things didn't get much better. Koosman was having arm trouble. The other young pitchers were not doing well, either. Only Jones was hitting. Hodges tried to maintain his poise. "We had good pitching last year," he said. "These are the same guys, I just can't see any reason why they shouldn't be doing the same thing."

But on May 15, the Mets stumbled to their eighth one-run defeat. The manager exploded. During the game, pitcher Cardwell had hurried a throw to second and tossed the ball into center field. Base runner Shamsky had foolishly tried to stretch a double and been thrown out by ten feet at third base. Gil slammed the clubhouse door and stared icily at the players. "I won't tolerate mental errors," he snapped. "Some of you are lackadaisical and complacent. We could be a first-division club. But we can't afford these mistakes."

The team responded by boosting its record to the .500 level. Then it slumped again. In late May the Mets were pounded into a 15-3 defeat by the Atlanta Braves, then lost four more games in a row.

Suddenly, almost unbelievably, the Mets came alive again. Led by Seaver and the rest of the revived pitching staff, they defeated San Diego and went on to sweep six straight from the Dodgers and Giants. By the first week in June they were in second place, ahead of the sagging Cardinals. "The old Mets are dead, baby," Agee cried. "Long live the new Mets."

The new Mets won eleven in a row. They challenged the first-place Cubs. No one viewed the Mets as serious pennant contenders, however, until they met the Cubs in six games during a nine-day period in early July. The first series opened at Shea Stadium with Chicago still five and a half games ahead.

The Cubs had a veteran team which had been in pennant fights before. Their lineup glittered with standouts like catcher Randy Hundley, third baseman Ron Santo, shortstop Don Kessinger, first baseman Ernie Banks, rightfielder Billy Williams, and two fine pitchers, Ken Holtzman and Ferguson Jenkins. The Chicagoans were unimpressed by the inexperienced, light-hitting Mets. Santo, the Cubs' captain, predicted that New York would fold when confronted with real pressure. "It'll get to them," he said. "They don't know what it is yet. We do."

But it was the Cubs who showed the first effects of pennant pressure. New York took advantage of a pair of misplays by Chicago's rookie center fielder, Don Young, and scored three runs in the last of the ninth to win, 4-3. After the game, Santo lost his composure. "Young took us down to defeat," he rasped. "He was brooding about his hitting instead of thinking about those fly balls." Santo apologized the next day. But by then Chicago had other problems. In the second inning, Santo and Kessinger made back to back errors as the Mets scored twice. The big story, however, was Tom Seaver. For eight innings he pitched perfect baseball. In the ninth, Chicago's crafty manager, Leo Durocher, ordered Hundley to lay down a surprise bunt. But Seaver bounded off the mound, fielded the ball and threw him out. Tom was just two outs away from a perfect game.

The next batter was Jim Qualls, a rookie who had played in only eighteen big league games. He was in the lineup because Durocher was angry at Young. The Mets didn't know how to pitch to Qualls.

Seaver threw a tailing fastball, intended to be low and away. But it got too close to the middle of the plate. Qualls sliced it to left center for a clean single. On the mound Seaver whispered, "Oh, no." His shoulders sagged and he stood in silence. Then the crowd rose and gave him a long, loud standing ovation. Tom quickly retired the last two hitters. The Mets won the second game, 4-0.

The Mets played terribly in the final game at New York, though, and lost, 6-2. After the game, Durocher crowed, "Those were the *real* Mets."

When the New Yorkers invaded Chicago a few days later, the Cubs nipped Seaver, 1-0, in the first game. But the Mets came back strong. Light-hitting Al Weis slammed a three-run homer to give the Mets a 5-4 victory. He had hit only four other homers in his seven-year career. The next day, Agee, Shamsky, and—of all people—Weis smacked homers and the Mets won again. Hodges praised his team's winning spirit. "I'll tell you what's happening out there," he said. "It's an epidemic. It's contagious. One guy's picking up the others. You never know who's going to do it next."

By the All-Star break in mid-July the Mets were breathing down the neck of the Cubs. The New Yorkers had won thirty-five of fifty-one games. They were the biggest sports story in the country. But after the All-Star game it seemed as if the youngsters were taking their press clippings a little too seriously. With eighty games left to play, they returned to their old, blundering style. On July 31, at Shea Stadium, the Astros twice humilated them, putting together an eleven-run ninth inning in the

first game and a ten-run third inning in the night-
cap. At one point Jones made a half-hearted effort
to chase a ball hit to left field. Suddenly Hodges
came out of the dugout and headed toward his star.
Everyone in the stadium watched in surprise as
Hodges went to the outfield. "Are you hurt?" Gil
snapped. "You must be hurt." Jones looked at the
ground in shame. Then Hodges waved to the dugout for an immediate replacement and led the embarrassed Jones back to the bench. The Mets remembered to hustle from then on.

But they didn't start winning immediately. On
August 9, they lost their third straight at the Houston Astrodome and fell nine and a half games behind the Cubs. St. Louis took over second place.
The impossible dream was becoming a nightmare.

But as quickly as they had fallen apart, the Mets
pulled themselves together. Seaver, who had been
bothered by a sore shoulder, returned to top form.
Boswell, Shamsky and Agee got hot at the plate.
The Mets won nine of ten games from the West
Coast teams. "We've come back from the dead
again," said Ed Kranepool.

Chicago had taken for granted that it would win
the pennant. Now the Cubs' huge lead was evapo-
rating. By September 8, when Chicago marched
into Shea Stadium for two vital games, Seaver had
already become a twenty-game winner and the
Mets were just two and a half games behind. But
the Cubs were still talking and acting tough. Chicago players predicted again that the Mets would
fold. And in the last half of the first inning, Cub
pitcher Bill Hands fired a high, tight fastball that

sent Agee sprawling. The pitch was meant to intimidate the Mets. It didn't. Koosman retaliated. He drilled a fastball that hit Santo's wrist. Agee answered the Cubs, too, with a two-run homer and a double. The double came in the sixth inning, with the score 2-2. It was actually just a soft liner to the left. But when the Chicago outfielder took his time fielding the ball, Tommie dashed for second and slid in, head first, ahead of the throw. Later he scored the winning run.

The next evening the Mets humilated Chicago. Seaver handcuffed the Chicago hitters. By the sixth inning, with the Mets leading 7-1, the happy fans began to taunt Leo Durocher with a chorus of "goodbye Leo" amidst a backdrop of waving handkerchiefs. It was Chicago's sixth loss in a row. The Mets were just two percentage points out of first place.

The next night was a big one in Met history. They defeated the Expos twice while Chicago was losing to Philadelphia. For the first time ever, the Mets were in first place. The New York fans left Shea Stadium chanting, "We're Number One."

That weekend in Pittsburgh, New York faced yet another crisis situation. Cleon Jones was out of the lineup with an injured rib. Boswell, who had hit .473 in the past eighteen games, was on weekend military duty. Shamsky, batting .303, could not play because he was observing a Jewish holiday. To further complicate matters, Pittsburgh had one of the hardest-hitting teams in baseball. So how did the Mets respond? Both Koosman and Cardwell pitched 1-0 victories in a doubleheader! And how did the Mets get their runs? Each pitcher knocked one in! In a tight 1-1 game the next day, Swoboda slammed a grand-slam home run in the eighth inning to insure a Met victory.

The Cubs, meanwhile, were on a binge that would see them lose ten of eleven games. The New Yorkers rolled happily along. Even when St. Louis Cardinal pitcher Steve Carlton struck out nineteen Mets to set a big-league record, the Mets won the game! On September 24, the team clinched at least a tie for first place. There were six games left. All the Mets needed was one victory.

The next evening 54,928 fans jammed Shea Stadium. They had come to celebrate. And celebrate they did. The Mets broke the game open in the first inning when Clendenon blasted a 410-foot, three-run homer. Charles hit a two-run homer. After the last out, Shea Stadium became a madhouse of joy.

In the clubhouse, the players yelled and stomped. They guzzled champagne, or poured and squirted it over each other. The celebration was led, appropriately, by Seaver and Koosman.

A week later the Mets finished their season with an even 100 victories and entered the best-of-five playoffs against the Atlanta Braves. Again they were underdogs—but they were confident underdogs. Their hopes, almost everyone agreed, depended on how well their fine pitchers harnessed the Braves' awesome power.

As it turned out, the New Yorkers' pitching was awful. Seaver was shelled for five runs in the first game. But the Mets won, 9-5. The next day, Koos-

Tom Seaver celebrates the Mets' pennant-clinching victory.

man blew a 9-1 lead and needed relief help. Still, New York won, 11-6.

The third game was played at Shea Stadium. A capacity crowd came out to watch the Mets win their first pennant. But Atlanta jumped on Gary Gentry in the first and third innings, building up a 2-0 lead. Hodges had seen enough. With two men on base, he waved to the bullpen for Nolan Ryan.

The young fastballer began firing strikes. He fanned one man, then walked Orlando Cepeda to load the bases. With the Mets in jeopardy of falling far behind, Ryan got the side out. The Mets were still alive. Moments later, Agee homered. In the next inning Art Shamsky singled and Ken Boswell homered to send New York in front, 3-2. Atlanta rallied for two runs off Ryan in the fifth, but the Mets came back once more. Ryan, who had gotten only three hits all season, singled. Wayne Garrett, who had not hit a homer in five months, smacked a pitch over the right field wall. The Mets were in front to stay. Nolan struck out seven in seven innings of great relief pitching. In the ninth, the crowd was roaring "Let's Go Mets." At 3:34 PM Ryan got Tony Gonzales to hit a grounder to Garrett at third. Garrett threw to Kranepool. The Mets, losers of 737 games in seven seasons, won the game and the pennant.

Once more the fans ripped up the field. Once more the players bathed in champagne in the clubhouse.

Understandably, the Mets were underdogs going into the World Series. Their opponents, the Baltimore Orioles, had won 109 games during the regular American League season and were considered one of the best baseball teams in years. They proved it by sweeping three straight playoff games from the Minnesota Twins.

On paper, the Oriole personnel seemed superior to the Mets. Outfielders Frank Robinson and Paul Blair, third baseman Brooks Robinson, and first baseman "Boog" Powell had combined for 118 home runs in 1969. The entire New York team had hit just 109. The Orioles' team batting average was .265, some twenty-three points better than the Mets. Although the Mets might claim superior pitching with Seaver and Koosman and all the depth, the Orioles' staff had two twenty-game winners of their own in Mike Cuellar and Dave McNally, plus some other strong arms. Besides, the Mets' top hurlers had problems: Seaver was suffering from a strained leg muscle and Koosman had developed a bad cold. Jim Russo, the Orioles' chief scout, frankly reported: "We respect the Mets' pitchers, but we should wrap this thing up in four or five games."

Since Cuellar and McNally, the Baltimore aces, were both left-handers, Hodges decided to use his right-handed hitting platoon when they were on the mound. That meant removing Shamsky, Boswell, and Garrett, three of the Mets' hottest batters, from the lineup. Charles would be at third, Clendenon at first, Swoboda in right field, and Weis at second for the opening game.

In the Series opener in Baltimore, the Orioles pounded Seaver for six hits and four runs in the first five innings. Meanwhile, Brooks Robinson made several sensational fielding plays and the Mets' right-handed platoon was ineffective against Cuellar. The Orioles won easily, 4-1. After the game, Frank Robinson needled the Mets by saying, "I looked at their bench in the seventh inning when they had the bases loaded and a chance to get back in the game. There was absolutely no cheering or enthusiasm. More than likely, the home run by Don Buford in the first inning took the heart right out of them."

But just when the Mets should have been at their lowest ebb, Jerry Koosman picked them up. Pitching brilliantly and receiving great help in the field, especially from Ed Charles, Koosman no-hit the Orioles for six innings of the second game. The Orioles, however, got a run in the seventh to make the score 1-1. It stayed that way until the ninth as the Orioles' McNally dueled Koosman strike for strike.

Then with two out, Charles bounced a single into left field. The Oriole fans had little reason for concern, though, since weak hitters like Grote and Weis were coming up next. But Grote also smacked a single and Charles, churning his 36-year-old legs with the pitch, steamed into third. Up to the plate came Weis, with his not-so-mighty .215 average. Hodges could have sent in a pinch hitter. But he didn't. Weis lined McNally's first pitch into left field for a single, scoring Charles. The Mets stopped Baltimore in the bottom of the inning to win, 2-1. Their first World Series victory was in the books.

The Series moved to New York, where Tommie Agee, who had done little in the Series, began to shine. Agee led off for the Mets in the third game by blasting a home run. An inning later, pitcher Gary Gentry, a poor hitter, lined a two-run double over Blair's head in center field. The Mets led, 3-0.

Baltimore threatened in the fourth inning, loading the bases with one out. Gentry clenched his teeth and struck out Brooks Robinson. Then catcher Elrod Hendricks blasted a long drive to deep left-center. It appeared to be an easy triple, which would tie the score. But Agee flashed across the outfield grass, arm outstretched, and snatched the ball in the webbing of his glove. He bounced off the wall, 396 feet from home plate. The crowd was screaming. It was one of the greatest catches in Series history.

Agee's miracle catches, like this one in the fourth game of the World Series, unnerved the favored Baltimore Orioles.

By the seventh inning the Mets led, 4-0, but Gentry was tiring. He walked three men in a row. Hodges went to the mound and called for Nolan Ryan to come in from the bullpen. Nolan poured two quick strikes past Blair. Then the Baltimore center fielder drove a fast ball deep to right-center. Again Agee made a desperate rush. At the last moment he dove for the ball as it began sinking to the ground. If he had missed it, the speedy Blair might have had an inside-the-park grand slam homer. But Tommie made a skidding, one-handed catch as he sprawled full length on the ground. The catch was even greater than his first one. The crowd of Met rooters first looked in disbelief, then gave Tommie a standing ovation. The Mets won, 5-0. The pressure was now clearly on Baltimore. And the pressure increased in the fourth game, everything went New York's way—a gritty performance by Seaver, a home run by Clendenon, a diving catch by Swoboda, a misjudged fly ball, and an umpire's oversight.

Going into the ninth inning, Clendenon's second inning homer was the only score of the game as the crowd of 57,367 cheered Seaver's every pitch. The Oriole offense was so shackled that Baltimore had been shut out for nineteen straight innings and had had just one run to show for thirty-one innings. But the ninth was rough for the Mets. Frank Robinson lashed a single with one out. Boog Powell singled, sending Robinson to third. Brooks Robinson then ripped a low, sinking liner to right-center. Swoboda raced over and dove for the ball in a desperate gamble. If he had missed, two runs surely would have scored. But Ron made a tumbling, backhanded catch. While Frank Robinson scored the tying run when he tagged up at third and beat Swoboda's throw to the plate, the Orioles' victory threat had been stifled. The game went into the tenth inning with the score 1-1.

In the bottom of the tenth, the angel of good fortune, which had hovered over the Mets all season, was still there. Grote hit an easy fly ball to left. But Buford lost the ball in the sun, enabling Grote to pull into second with a double. Weis was walked intentionally to set up a possible double play. Then J. C. Martin, a reserve catcher, batted for the tiring Seaver. Hodges ordered Martin to lay down a sac-

rifice bunt. The bunt was perfect, stopping down
the first base line about ten feet from the plate.

As Rod Gaspar, running for Grote, galloped to
third, Oriole pitcher Pete Richert grabbed the
bunted ball and threw hurriedly to first. But his
throw struck Martin in the wrist and bounced
toward right field. The Orioles were helpless as
Gaspar came home with the winning run. It was not
until photos of the play were developed that anyone
noticed that Martin had run inside the baseline on
his way to first. J.C. should have been called out
and the run should have been nullified. But the
umpires had missed the call. The magical Mets
were one victory away from the World Championship.

The next day Baltimore scored three runs in the
third inning against Koosman, as McNally and
Frank Robinson homered. But by now it seemed as
though a Mets' victory was inevitable. The team
could do no wrong. In the sixth inning the Mets
began to move. Clendenon hit a two-run homer,
his third of the series. In the seventh, Weis tied the
game with a home run, raising his series batting av
erage to .454. Even mild-mannered Al was surprised by the blast. "When I got near second," he
said later, "I started to hear the crowd roar and
thought something must have happened. I guess I
don't know how to react to a home run."

Meanwhile Koosman was stifling the Orioles. In
the eighth, with the score 3-3, Jones lined a double
off the centerfield fence. Swoboda doubled to left,
scoring Jones with what proved to be the winning
run. The crowd was in a frenzy. Swoboda scored

Manager Gil Hodges receives congratulations from grizzly Casey Stengel, who used the phrase "Amazin' Mets" when it meant losing, not winning.

with two out when Powell booted Grote's grounder. The Mets moved into the ninth with a 5-3 lead.

In a moment, it was all over. The Orioles went down quickly and easily in the ninth inning to end the game. The Mets were world champions!

The fans could not restrain themselves. For the third time during the season, they tore the field to pieces. They danced and sang and proudly stuck their forefingers in the air, signifying "We're Number One." Throughout the city of New York, masses of people celebrated, too. The streets of Manhattan were filled with tons of ticker tape or whatever people felt like dumping out of skyscraper office buildings. A bus driver stopped collecting fares. And a partying mood began that lasted well into the night.

Meanwhile, back at Shea Stadium, the players shouted or wept with joy. Champagne was squirted freely between drinks. In the noisy locker room, manager Hodges could hardly hear the voice of President Richard Nixon, who called to offer his congratulations. The best description of the players' mood was offered by aging Ed Charles, who would be taking off his Met uniform for the last time. Charles said simply, "This is the summit. We're number one in the world and you just can't get any bigger than that."

Index